Inspired by the Modern Homesteading movement, Bella and Nick Ivins left the city behind and relocated to an idyllic smallholding in rural Sussex to embrace a home-based, family-centred and self-sufficient way of life. Rather than being slaves to the land, the couple were determined to make homesteading work for them, learning on the job, giving everything a go, and vowing to do 'just enough and nothing more'. *Living the Country Dream* tells the story of life on Walnut covering every a kitchen gard and preservin want to start your own homestead, whether in the city, the country or the suburbs, and aim to become fully or partly self-sufficient, *Living the Country Dream* provides the knowledge necessary and puts the dream within reach.

# LIVING THE COUNTRY DREAM

# LIVING THE COUNTRY DREAM

How to create a self-sufficient homestead,
grow your own produce and raise livestock

## Bella & Nick Ivins

*With photography by* Nick Ivins

RYLAND PETERS & SMALL
LONDON • NEW YORK

First published in 2016 as
*The New Homesteader*.
This edition published in 2021 by
Ryland Peters & Small
20–21 Jockey's Fields,
London WC1R 4BW
and
341 East 116th Street,
New York NY 10029

www.rylandpeters.com

10 9 8 7 6 5 4 3 2 1

Text © Bella and Nick Ivins
2016, 2021
Design © Ryland Peters & Small
2016, 2021
Photography © Nick Ivins
2016, 2021

ISBN: 978-1-78879-355-1

Printed and bound in China

A CIP record for this book is
available from the British
Library.

US Library of Congress
Cataloging-in-Publication Data
has been applied for.

*Senior Designer* Toni Kay
*Senior Commissioning Editor*
 Annabel Morgan
*Head of Production* Patricia Harrington
*Art Director* Leslie Harrington
*Editorial Director* Julia Charles
*Publisher* Cindy Richards

# Contents

# Introduction

Over the ten years we have spent here at Walnuts Farm, we have developed a system of food production that suits us as well as the land we farm. Our aim as homesteaders is to raise just the right amount to feed our little family and any visiting friends, but no more. We don't aim for a surplus or to sell produce at a profit. It is also important to point out that we are not 100 per cent self-sufficient or purist about trying to be so. We admire those homesteaders who are both, but for us it is simply a question of growing what we like to eat, is expensive to buy or tastes best fresh from the garden. We are not ashamed to head to the grocery store, a local farm shop or even the supermarket to augment our produce. You could perhaps call us fair-weather farmers, in that we aim to put in the least effort for maximum enjoyment and optimal production from the resources we have available.

When we started out, we soon discovered that to succeed as homesteaders, it's essential to work with what you've got rather than fight against it. Walnuts Farm is situated on heavy clay and poor and unimproved grazing land. Because of the wet conditions over winter, we can only rear livestock outdoors during the summer months. For us, therefore, most of our homesteading activities take place in this season. We do less farming in the winter months and more hunting for game foods. Winter is also a time to warm by the fireside, to rest, take stock and plan for the year to come.

In this book, we hope to show how you too can make a virtue of necessity, whatever the scope of your enterprise. And also to prove that the good life does not have to be the hard life. Whether you 'farm' on a microscale in an urban backyard or suburban garden, or upon several rural acres, or even if the notion of homesteading is still a dream rather than a reality, we hope that our experiences, successes and failures will be of interest. If your desire is to become totally self-sufficient, then our method of homesteading offers an easy way in and a place from which to expand.

We decided from the start that everything at Walnuts Farm has to 'feed the eye as well as the family', for our aim is to gain as much pleasure from the doing as from the final result. We are conscious that our homesteading is to some extent a labour of love and as such must reward us in every way. This is not, for us, a luxury. With every activity we have an opportunity to do it well and to find an elegant design solution, or to merely do it adequately, at a cost to the environment and to aesthetics.

On our homestead, we have several different enterprises separated into distinct zones. Adjacent to the house, the kitchen garden is at the heart of the enterprise. We find that it is best positioned close to the house as we work in it little and often, sowing, growing and harvesting throughout the year. Surrounding this are areas for pigs, sheep, bees and poultry, on the meadows and among the woodland. These enterprises require less of our labour so can be positioned a little further from the house.

Despite what non-gardening visitors may think, our kitchen garden is relatively easy to manage. Most of our fruit and vegetable production takes place on less than an acre. We do not dig our beds as we're on clay, and in our experience this is best left below ground and not

brought to the surface. But our growing beds are big – approximately 7.5 x 7.5m/25 x 25ft each. Between them we have laid hard-wearing gravel paths that fit a wide wheelbarrow, and the central axis will accommodate a Land Rover plus trailer. We don't try to extend the growing season at either end, as we have limited resources and no polytunnel. Accordingly, we outsource some early seed-growing to a friend's commercial glasshouses nearby, and this gives us a head start on the growing year.

When we are tilling the ground, we have to work efficiently. We use a big cultivator hoe for weeding and so we plant rows to fit the width of the cultivator. We use few other tools and spend little time watering as we are growing for flavour, not volume. We do spend time on defence – keeping rabbits and deer out, as well as mice and slugs – but at least we can harvest some of these pests for the kitchen table.

We introduce pigs and lambs as young stock in spring, when the land dries out, and fatten them up over summer, using as much home-grown grass and feed as possible. They are all in the freezer by the time the land becomes wet again in autumn. The animals have complemented the vegetable and fruit production and integrated well with it, as well as providing interest and pleasure both in everyday life and on the plate. If we started over again, we would use pigs and chickens to do more of the site-clearing, and integrate the pigs directly into the rotation of beds in the kitchen garden to prepare the beds for cultivation.

This is the story of our easy way into homesteading, trying out a variety of different enterprises while keeping our set-up and labour costs as low as possible. Every year is different and we have had our fair share of failures as well as successes, but this is part of what keeps us interested and the reason we operate multiple enterprises. There are always some surprise successes to make up for the inevitable failures. The land and livestock work hard for us, and fit in around our other jobs.

What of the rewards? Well, there is fabulous food, the like of which is hard to buy even at the premium 'organic' end of the market, and a lifestyle that 'feeds the eye as well as the family'. Above all, the greatest pleasure is, without a doubt, producing by one's own hand and endeavour the food for one's family. It is an act of love that undoubtedly appeals to the hunter and gatherer within us all.

# THE
# KITCHEN
# GARDEN

THIS PAGE AND OPPOSITE *It was part of our original plan for the kitchen garden that each of the vegetable beds would be surrounded by evergreen box/boxwood hedging* (Buxus sempervirens) *to give the plot a pleasing year-round formality. However, we made the mistake of not planting the young box plants close enough together. Not only were rabbits getting in, but we didn't have the structured look we'd imagined. We have remedied this in two ways: firstly, by erecting a low rabbit-proof wire fence around the perimeter of each bed, and secondly, by infilling the hedges with small box cuttings bought at a local plant auction. Several years on, we now have a seamless hedge around all four beds (opposite).*

# Planning the Kitchen Garden

*Our kitchen garden sits on the north side of the farmhouse and is only a stone's throw from the kitchen door. It is the focus of all our efforts outdoors, and we have purposely designed it so that it is permanently 'on show' from the house and something to celebrate. Every single day, we delight in the beauty of this productive piece of garden that feeds the eye as well as the stomach.*

Many people might imagine that a patch of land for growing fruit and vegetables is best placed at the bottom of the garden, tucked out of sight, but our kitchen garden is at the heart of the homestead. Our ambition is to grow and eat fresh ingredients throughout the year and we treat the kitchen garden as our walk-in larder. We pick our produce as and when we need it. We don't store fresh ingredients in the salad drawer in the refrigerator or in a vegetable rack as we like to eat everything 'superfood' fresh. We simply pop outside to cut a few stems of broccoli and pick a handful of beans to steam for supper – a real treat. A kitchen garden encourages the family cook to be resourceful with the available produce and harvest 'just enough', so that nothing goes to waste. Some crops will fail, while others will be too successful, and the clever thing is to know how to deal with either situation.

## GETTING STARTED

When it comes to planning a kitchen garden, be ambitious but don't imagine every inch has to be super-productive – you're not a commercial farmer. Give your kitchen garden a structure, using low hedging and espaliered fruit trees to divide the space. If you are on poor soil or heavy clay (like us), don't dig down but opt for a raised bed system instead. Follow the orientation of the house when laying out the garden, so the two form an integrated whole. We plant in squares rather than rows, as they are visually more pleasing. We also plant crops along a north–south axis rather than east–west, so that they get the maximum amount of daylight and aren't cast in their own shadow. Gravel paths, just wider than a wheelbarrow, are laid throughout the garden so we can step out from the back door and keep our feet mud-free, even when it's very wet.

LEFT *To add height to the kitchen garden, we coppice long hazel poles from the nuttery and tie three or four together with hop-growers' string to make simple wigwams. These are renewed each year, as by the end of a long, dry summer the poles become brittle and snap easily. We make a couple of wigwams for each of the four beds and grow a mix of climbing flowers and vegetables up their poles. Squash plants love to climb, as do sweet peas and nasturtiums (shown here). Our intention is for the kitchen garden to look pretty as well as be productive.*

ABOVE *In late autumn our garlic seed bulbs arrive by post. Each individual clove is then planted out in plugs and put in the cold frame. A few weeks later, green shoots appear and we transplant the young garlic plants into the 'root' bed*

alongside onions, shallots and leeks. We water them in as soon as we've planted a block of plants to give them a good start. Interestingly, garlic needs a spell of frost to help the cloves divide and then they look after themselves until their high-summer harvest.

OPPOSITE *Sweetcorn/corn is best planted out in blocks rather than rows as they need to wind-pollinate themselves to produce the cobs. The plants grow tall by late summer and you know the cobs are ready to pick when their beards start turning brown. Varieties such as 'Sweet Nugget' are almost good enough to eat straight from the plant, but dropped into a pan of boiling water and eaten with butter or black pepper, they are like nothing you've ever tasted. If there is one vegetable to grow and eat fresh and seasonal, this is it!*

LEFT *We grow two varieties of espaliered dessert pear trees, Doyenné du Comice and Beurre Hardy, both of which were bought as spindly maidens. They are now five years old and, with judicious training along strands of galvanized steel wire tied to chestnut poles, the four layers of espaliered pear branches maximize the vertical growing space. Pear trees flower earlier than apple, so in early spring a wave of blossom comes into flower along the central avenue of the kitchen garden, providing welcome early forage for flying insects.*

BELOW *During the winter months, the framework that* supports the espaliered trees catches the frost and sparkles in the pale sunshine, as do the split-chestnut gates and the woven-willow fencing, adding visual interest when there is little growing.

OPPOSITE *The traditional time of year to harvest willow for fence-making is at the end of the growing season. The straight, flexible stems are perfect for weaving of all types, but for fence-making we select the thicker, two-year-old poles, which are about about 5cm/2in in diameter. The thinner leafy tops are sliced off with a billhook – satisfying outdoor work on a winter's day.*

## CREATING STRUCTURE AND HEIGHT

Our kitchen garden started out as a flat, bare site and over the years our aim has been to add as much height and structure as possible. It's like building a 3-D sculpture as it involves a process of layering, which takes time – this is not instant gardening. Now, ten years on, this vertical and horizontal framework not only provides shade and shelter, but also a scaffold for vegetable and plant matter to grow up. We have introduced pleached lime trees (*Tilia cordata*, also known as little-leaf linden), espaliered dessert pear and apple trees, and box hedging for this purpose, and the whole kitchen garden is enclosed in woven-willow fencing, which adds a sculptural quality. This structure gives the kitchen garden 'good bones', which are particularly evident during winter months when the garden is laid bare.

# Making woven-willow fencing

During one of those crisp days between Christmas and the end of the winter season, we head down to the willow plantation and, armed with loppers, pruning saws and billhooks, harvest the two-year-old willow growth. By this stage, the stems are thumb thick and about as much as the loppers can comfortably slice through. We bundle up the 2.4-3.6m/8-12ft poles, lash them together and carry them back up to the garden.

Before fence-making, we will have already erected a row of chest-high sweet chestnut spiles (or posts) in the line that the new fence is to take. The first spile is driven into the ground at one end of the proposed fence, and the second and subsequent spiles are placed at regular intervals, determined by placing the elbow atop the first spile and driving the second where the hand holding it naturally falls.

The hazel bundles are dropped alongside the line of posts at right angles for easy access, and then it's a case of weaving them around the spiles, working from one end and starting with the thick heal of each rod. It's rather like basketry on a large scale. You can make your fence messy or neat, but either way aim for a good, tight weave so the fence is strong enough to bear a man's weight. Willow fencing will age over time and eventually become dry and brittle, but it should last as long as a hedge planted to grow alongside it takes to fill out and replace it. In our case, it's five to eight years before the weave needs replacing.

# Common Kitchen Garden Pests

*Although box/boxwood hedging shelters our vegetable beds and provides year-round evergreen structure, it does have a downside in that it harbours pests, providing shelter for snails and slugs.*

Before the hedging grew to a reasonable height, our main problem was rabbits decimating the young crops, so we ring-fenced each vegetable bed with chicken wire held in place by split chestnut posts 1m/3ft high. The wire is now covered by the box but it accounts for the less-than-perfect edges – our hedging leans towards a 'cloud' formation, as over time the chicken-wire structure beneath has bent and sagged in places, making the hedging difficult to cut in straight lines. We have never been brave enough to remove the chicken wire completely for fear of rabbits squeezing through the tiniest of gaps in the hedge.

Pigeons descend onto the beds both morning and evening to nibble at the tender tops of purple sprouting broccoli or other young brassicas, while at night a whole raft of pests make their presence known. Perhaps the best way to deal with them is to grow enough produce for it to not be a problem when they consume some of your crop. Interfering tends to upset the natural order of things, so we only use chemical powder to combat the cabbage white butterfly and rely on toads or our ducks to do some of the slug and snail removal.

We also try to avoid attracting pests of all kinds by not sowing seeds directly into the soil too early in the year. Instead, we start off most of our young plants under cover (see pages 28–29). Chances are that seeds planted early, such as broad/fava beans and peas, will be eaten by mice, while slugs feast upon the juicy leaves and stems of young seedlings. We circumvent these problems by buying in young stock from a local nursery that belongs to a friend. They grow some unusual vegetable varieties from seed there and we collect them when they are ready to plant out. That way, our time can be better spent elsewhere on the homestead.

OPPOSITE ABOVE LEFT *Black mesh is stapled onto makeshift square frames to keep birds off tender green leaves during their long growing season. The frames are lightweight and can be moved easily by two people.*

OPPOSITE ABOVE RIGHT *Early on in the making of the kitchen garden we had to install chicken wire around the outer edge of each growing bed to keep the rabbits out. Long plastic cloches offer a second line of defence against the elements for young plants.*

OPPOSITE BELOW *In our efforts to repel predators, we have also chicken-wired all our cleft chestnut gates and our first soft fruit area (on the left of the photo). In fact, chicken wire underpins most of the kitchen garden's structure, and who knows if we would have much growing there without it!*

ABOVE *The devastation wrought by the dreaded cabbage white caterpillar can be seen here. In the space of a few days the leaves of this brassica have been stripped bare.*

# Growing Herbs

*We grow our favourite herbs — flat-leaf parsley, sweet basil and chives — in the kitchen garden alongside the vegetables, rather than in a dedicated herb garden. This way the herbs enjoy rich soil, light and space, and are not overshadowed by large perennial herbs, such as rosemary.*

The basil and parsley produce an abundant harvest of fresh leaves throughout the summer months when grown on a large scale and really thrive in the space, producing large bushy plants. They form the mainstay of our summer lunches and suppers, and there is nothing like being able to harvest huge armfuls of fresh herbs to add to a simple pasta sauce with finely chopped garlic and anchovies. Our local greengrocer sells huge bunches of herbs at reasonable prices, which are far superior to the supermarket stalks packaged in plastic or the pot-grown herbs, which are often grown hydroponically, resulting in flaccid, relatively tasteless leaves. Grow your own on a grand scale and you will never look back.

LEFT *We sow parsley from tiny, fiddly seed, rinsing it first in warm water to kick-start germination. Harvest stalks several times to encourage new shoots. At the end of the season, dig it up to start afresh next year.*

BELOW *We cut the chives back hard when the flowers start to dry out, to be rewarded with a second crop of juicy stalks. Its strong oniony scent deters pests like carrot fly.*

# Spanish omelette

Bella's mother was born and raised in Barcelona and makes the best Spanish omelette. To bring out the lovely mix of flavours, serve just warm or cold the next day, or as tapas with a glass of sherry at the end of the working day.

50g/3 tablespoons salted butter

1 large onion, finely sliced

3 garlic cloves, finely sliced

500g/1lb 2oz potatoes, peeled and sliced

6–8 eggs, beaten

generous handful of flat-leaf parsley, chopped

rock salt and freshly ground black pepper

Melt the butter in a large frying pan/skillet over a gentle heat. Add the onions and soften them, then add the garlic, taking care not to let it burn. Meanwhile, parboil the potato slices for 10 minutes in a pan of salted, boiling water. Drain the potato slices and add to the onion and garlic. Pour the beaten eggs over the mixture and sprinkle with parsley. Season with salt and pepper. Cook over a gentle heat for 10 minutes, until the base of the omelette is cooked.

Meanwhile, preheat the grill/broiler. Place the pan under the grill/broiler to cook the top of the omelette. Using a non-stick spatula, loosen the omelette and turn out onto a serving plate or board. Leave to cool. Cut into slices and serve lukewarm or cold.

# Making horseradish sauce

I was taught that the definition of a herb is a plant that is both useful or medicinal, and horseradish, which is known for its anti-inflammatory properties, fits the bill. After several failed attempts at cultivating it in the heart of the kitchen garden, it now grows well alongside the compost heap, together with the Jerusalem artichokes.

We dig up the roots in autumn when the flavour is strongest and use them fresh for extra potency. Fresh horseradish sauce served with roast beef or oily fish, such as mackerel, is hard to beat. Once dug, the roots will keep in the refrigerator if you scrub them and wrap them in a plastic bag.

Here's our simple recipe for fresh horseradish sauce – you can adjust quantities to suit your tastebuds.

horseradish root, scrubbed,
  peeled and grated

crème fraîche or double/heavy
  cream

1 teaspoon English mustard

salt and freshly ground black
  pepper

freshly squeezed lemon juice

Once peeled and grated, quickly mix the horseradish with the other ingredients to prevent it from discolouring. You want a lovely creamy consistency, so mix in plenty of crème fraîche (or double/heavy cream, if you prefer your sauce to be richer). Then add a teaspoon of mustard, season with salt and pepper, and add lemon juice, to taste.

We also use horseradish sauce as the starting point for home-made smoked mackerel pâté, mashing two smoked, skinned mackerel fillets into the horseradish mix with a fork. Add a few more tablespoons of crème fraîche or cream to taste.

RIGHT AND FAR RIGHT *Garlic cloves are traditionally planted outdoors in late autumn, but we now start them off in modules under glass to increase the success rate (in the past dogs and garden birds pulled out the cloves before they had become established). Now we plant out garlic in the 'green'. Following the edge of a scaffolding board allows us to plant in a straight row without compacting wet soil.*

OPPOSITE *Grown under glass, chillies do surprisingly well here. We harvest the plants whole and hang them upside down to dry.*

ABOVE *Our pleasingly shaped terracotta rhubarb forcer raises young stalks in the dark, which results in a pale and tender crop, harvested in early spring.*

# Growing Under Cover

*Having under-cover outdoor space helps you get going a little earlier in the growing year and extends the seasons at either side, but if you're starting out, it is not a necessity.*

We've gone for many years without a polytunnel or glasshouse and just use cold frames to cover tender seedlings. We also use cloches to help salad crops to get off to a good start and as permanent cover for sweet basil, as this needs moist, warm conditions to grow well. Similarly, we use cloches for cultivating chillies as the warmth helps the fruits to ripen.

In the cold frame, check the undersides of seed trays and pots for slugs and snails. Don't forget to water the seedlings once they start to emerge (seed trays should not be watered too regularly before this point or the seeds may go mouldy and rot). We scrub out our cloches and glass domes at the start and end of the season with dishwashing liquid and a stiff brush to remove any diseases or algae that form on the surface of the glass and block the light. Greenhouse glass should be washed throroughly in a similar manner at the end of the season.

# The Shed

*The shed in our kitchen garden is the original garden shed from our first home, where it almost filled the tiny cottage garden. It was designed by Nick and engineered to a high specification, with heavy-duty galvanized metal hinges, lead guttering and a handmade clay peg-tiled roof. At the time it seemed a bit of an extravagance, but it has now served us well for ten years as a multifunctional space for storing garden tools and raising young livestock close to the house.*

ABOVE *Only our most useful kitchen garden tools hang in the shed as they are in daily use. These look like they have been put back without cleaning, but a quick dip in our deep box filled with sharp sand and vegetable oil is the most efficient way to tackle this.*

BELOW *The stable door works well for drying skins in good weather, and when we have livestock in*

residence, *it allows for good ventilation – an essential requisite of animal health. We have a grille that fits behind the door to prevent enthusiastic young lambs from jumping out.*

BELOW RIGHT *The shed is just a stone's throw from the kitchen so that in early spring we can keep an eye and ear out for our orphan lambs, who are housed there on a bed of straw.*

The shed was the first structure we erected when we arrived at Walnuts Farm. We knew exactly where it should go, and for many months it sat alone along the hedge line of the bare field site as we dreamed, planned and set about building and planting an ambitious kitchen garden around it.

The real appeal of the shed is that it is so close to the house and can be reached along the dry gravel paths in slippers or even just socks.

It functions as a shelter on rainy days, a dry store for hay and straw, and a tool store for the gardening implements that are in regular use. We hang our tools on pegs to keep the floor area clear of clutter, and keep their blades sharp and oiled after use by plunging them into a box filled with sharp sand and vegetable oil that sits in the corner – that's the theory anyway!

In spring, when the orphan lambs arrive, the sand box goes out and the water bucket moves in. We spread a bed of straw over the floor to make it comfortable for the lambs (and the children, who take up residence there). Nick has fitted a wooden baton to the back of the shed door so that the lambs' milk-bottle rack can be hung up all ready for feeding. In the winter months, when we don't have any livestock, we move in our pet guinea pigs' hutches and sometimes also the quail.

ABOVE *In autumn, the kitchen garden turns to orange and gold, as sweetcorn and squash ripen and nasturtiums and pot marigolds run riot. The shed acts as the holding bay for much of the harvested produce. Apple box after apple box are stacked high on top of one another, filled with loose onions and garlic before they are strung up. Squash are hung from the rafters in string nets to keep them rodent free, and drying beans are in trugs, waiting to be podded and stored in glass jars.*

**OPPOSITE ABOVE LEFT**
*Our Sussex trug has weathered well, and its balanced shape ensures it won't topple over as you toss fresh beans into its shallow curve. When not in use, it sits in the recesses of the bread oven, storing freshly dug potatoes in the dark to prevent them from turning green.*

**OPPOSITE ABOVE RIGHT**
*Bella loves watching her old French sprinkler come to life and the children shriek with laughter as they run through its path, enjoying any opportunity to get soaking wet. Bella discovered it in a local junk shop and it has proved to be a practical and beautiful solution to watering the kitchen garden during long, dry summers.*

**OPPOSITE BELOW LEFT**
*Our collecting bucket is made from recycled tyres and is the perfect size for weeding the beds and collecting leaves. We carry it into the beds and then tip its contents into the wheelbarrow as we work.*

**OPPOSITE BELOW RIGHT**
*The water bowser frame with its iron wheels was here when we moved to Walnuts Farm and we bought an old galvanized dustbin to fit it. We now use the bowser as it was intended, to collect and redistribute rainwater.*

**RIGHT** *Nick's work trousers/pants have a useful canvas loop that he uses as a holster, hanging his onion hoe there so it is always ready for action.*

# Essential Kitchen Garden Tools

*When it comes to tools, our priority is to invest in a few good-quality items that are versatile and can do many jobs. Bella's personal favourite is her Sneeboer ladies spade with its solid ash handle, as it is lightweight and has a sharp blade. It comes in useful for harvesting deep-rooted crops and weeds from our clay soil and is very nearly the perfect tree-planting spade.*

The other two implements that we use regularly are a small onion hoe and a large soil cultivator. An onion hoe is a traditional tool for weeding between onions within a row, but we frequently use it for other jobs too. It's ideal for preparing soil before sowing, drill making and digging a wedge before planting out seedlings. It is also handy for cleaning out animal hutches and hen houses, where its usefully angled head can scrape out even the darkest corners.

Our other essential is a large five-pronged soil cultivator. This fearsome-looking implement rips through weeds about five times faster than a hoe and makes turning a layer of soil easy work. We rely upon it so much that we now plant rows at a width to match that of the cultivator. Second-hand examples are hard to find and the ones we see are usually smaller, inferior versions. When ours finally succumbs to old age, we may have to get a new one made at our local blacksmiths.

Almost every other tool is secondary, with the exception of a good pair of secateurs or pruning shears and a sharpening stone. Strong secateurs make every angled slicing cut a pleasure.

Galvanized buckets and rubber trugs are perfect for transporting produce or weeds between the beds and the wheelbarrow, which should be large, strong enough to last through several seasons and preferably twin wheeled. This means it will carry more weight, spin effortlessly on its own axis, and require less heavy lifting.

We do like a power tool but the inevitable noise generated is problematic, especially on weekends. Having said that, our hedges are cut by a petrol hedge trimmer or a tractor-mounted equivalent which, although horribly noisy, has the advantage of mulching as it goes.

A backpack brush cutter is useful for tidying rough grass and its design saves the back as well as making it easy to manoeuvre beneath trees and hedges. And a mower is useful for cutting paths through the meadow. Ours has a good engine but inferior tinwork and is not a pleasure to use. At the end of the summer, parts from it are scattered all around the meadow – we discover them over winter and reattach a few. We are looking forward to replacing it with something more robust but, despite its shortcomings, it is proving remarkably resilient!

OPPOSITE AND ABOVE *Our five-pronged cultivator is as close as you can get to a tractor-drawn agricultural tool. It makes light work of turning the soil, lifting and hoeing weeds in its wake, while raking the dark topsoil to a fine tilth in preparation for planting out. It also has the added advantage of not disturbing the unwanted subsoil of clay. It has a really pleasing action – you simply lean into it, putting your weight on your front foot, and work*

*back and forth, letting the spade-shaped prongs slice through the ground and do the work.*

BELOW *Both aesthetically and ethically, we much prefer galvanized-metal containers, such as watering cans and chicken drinkers, to their plastic equivalents. The metal ages beautifully, developing a rich patina, whereas plastic discolours with age and gathers green slime when holding*

*water. A metal container is without doubt heavier to carry about the plot but is far more pleasing to the eye.*

BELOW RIGHT *Leaning up against the shed is one of the old millstones for Twissell Mill, the millrace of which can still be seen on the lower-lying neighbouring property, alongside the brook. We are not really sure how this heavy piece of heavy kit ended up here, but we like its solid beauty.*

# Practical Workwear

*Over the years, we've come to realize that good-quality workwear is worth paying for as it will keep you warm and dry in all weathers. We favour jerkins, waistcoats/vests, trousers/pants and dungarees made from hard-wearing natural fabrics that age well.*

When you're working outside, layers are essential. We start with a thermal undervest, followed by a long-sleeved cotton shirt for protection from thorns and biting insects, then a wool waistcoat or vest to keep the lower back and kidneys warm on a cold day. Nick owns three or four pairs of canvas work trousers/pants – they are his uniform. When new, they are as stiff as board and almost stand up by themselves, but with wear they fade and soften. Bella prefers the duck-bib overall version which, like Nick's trousers, only improve with wear.

Dry, warm feet are essential. Buy knee-high woollen socks – they dry much quicker than cotton ones. Invest in expensive wellington/rain boots – Bella's have lasted for 13 years of daily use, and she even wears them at the desk on cold days as they keep her feet warmer than slippers. We also recommend a sturdy pair of ankle boots with sheep's wool inner soles, as they can be slipped on and off easily when you're cooking and need to pop out to the garden. Waterproof clogs are useful too, as you can slip them on and kick them off at the back door.

Gloves and hats are key requirements of our homestead uniform. Bella likes kid-leather gardening gloves, but the fingertips do wear out in time. Felt hats with a wide brim offer good protection – choose one that fits well, so it won't blow off in a gust of wind.

ABOVE LEFT *Blue cotton men's dungarees from our agricultural store and ankle boots are Bella's summer uniform. Even though it is relatively dry underfoot, we still try not to walk on the beds, but kneel on planks to spread our weight.*

ABOVE CENTRE *Bella prefers kid-leather gardening gloves to the gauntlet style as they age well.*

ABOVE RIGHT *A scarf will keep the neck and chest warm in winter and perspiration-free in summer.*

OPPOSITE *It's easy to exercise the logic that clothing for outdoor use only should be cheap and throwaway, but in fact the reverse is true. If, like us, you're wearing work clothes most of the time, you want them to feel and look good.*

# THE
# ORCHARD

# Planning an Orchard and Growing Soft Fruit

*One of the easiest and most rewarding ways to grow your own food is by planting fruit trees and bushes. Once established, they require comparatively little management and the return in produce can be so great that sometimes we hardly know what to do with it all.*

It pays to establish an orchard early in the life of your homestead as it will take a few seasons to become truly productive. The trees can all go in during your first winter. We purchase 'maidens'—year-old bare-root trees — at auction or wholesale. These are field-grown and dug up and delivered in a dormant state during the winter. The maidens establish quickly, are easily trained and soon catch up with their expensive pot-grown cousins.

When it comes to planting your orchard, give some thought to how the trees will mature, positioning them carefully so that the taller will not overshadow the smaller and they all receive an equal blessing of sun and rain. We have planted on a north–south axis, with those trees anticipated to grow tallest positioned at the northern end. Where space is limited, such as within the kitchen garden, we have trained pear trees into espalier

OPPOSITE AND ABOVE *If you are lucky, you may receive a fruit tree or two as a 'house-warming' present - these pot-grown trees are a few years old and quickly come into fruit. Alternatively, 'maidens' will quickly establish and can be trained as you wish (assuming suitable rootstock). If you inherit a big, old apple tree, judicious pruning will ensure that fruit can be picked at a convenient height. Alternatively, you'll need a ladder, or an agile climber.*

forms. These create divisions within the garden and maximize the vertical growing space.

The orchard requires little attention for much of the year, so it can be established at some distance from the house but out of the shadow of larger broadleaved trees like oak and ash, which draw a lot of moisture from the soil. At first, we made the mistake of planting our orchard in the front meadow, close to large established trees, but when the apples, quinces and medlars failed to thrive, we moved it to a corner of the field that adjoins the kitchen garden. The fruit trees hated being moved and needed plenty of watering and mulching to bed them in, but now, several years on, the poultry and geese scratch happily around in the trees' shade, as do the lambs in summer.

As well as the orchard produce, we grow soft fruits and cherries. These need protection from birds, so we started off growing them in a cage made of chicken wire at the back of the kitchen garden, but it soon proved to be too small. Fruit bushes need more space than you think, and we like lots of produce, so one winter we pulled the cage down and moved the fruit out into the adjoining orchard field. Growing on a field basis can mitigate some of the loss of fruit to birds, but even so we have to net the ripening fruit for best results.

We grow other fruit trees, such as peach and morello cherry, against the house and garden walls. This was firstly because we wanted to benefit from the walls' heat-radiating qualities and secondly to put an otherwise unproductive north wall to good use.

FAR LEFT *Strawberries are a favourite with us, but also with the local blackbirds. We grow them in the fruit cage and in the vegetable beds, where they are protected by low, netted frames. The ripening fruits rest on straw, which stops them turning mouldy on the bare earth, but slug protection is needed too.*

LEFT *Currants – black, white and red – are easy to grow and, with a little autumn or winter pruning and protection from the birds during the fruiting season, can yield a great* quantity *from a relatively small space. Ours mostly go straight into the freezer for a hit of Vitamin C during long, dark winter months.*

ABOVE *Heavy-cropping loganberry bushes are enclosed within the fruit cage. Loganberries are a cross between blackberries and raspberries.*

OPPOSITE *Gooseberries freeze well. Ours are mostly used for winter desserts and in ice cream, but in midsummer, a gooseberry sauce with oily mackerel is not to be missed.*

OPPOSITE *These Laxton's Superb apples are developing well, but perhaps we should have thinned them to allow fewer, better fruit to develop. It is a balance between labour expended and yield of produce returned, and we tend to err on the side of minimal intervention as we're always busy doing other things. Nick's father was a specialist grower for horticultural shows, and took the opposite view, that no effort was too great to produce a small quantity of perfect produce.*

LEFT *Celluloid signage ensures that we remember what we have planted.*

## DECIDING WHAT TO GROW

When it comes to choosing what to grow in the orchard, we opt for fruit that we like to eat and that is hard to find or expensive to buy locally, as well as appealing new varieties and flavours.

Our staples are apples and pears. We enjoy the nutty Egremont Russet apple, and at a taste test at a local apple fair we sampled the crisp Cox-type Laxton's Superb and planted up accordingly. For pears, we have Beurre Hardy and Doyenné du Comice, both deliciously sweet dessert pears. To the mix we've added cherries, gages and plums, as well as Asian pears and the sublimely scented quince.

Soft fruit plants never last long and have to be regularly replaced, but we always grow plenty of raspberries of both summer and autumn types.

Currant bushes – black, white, red and Josta (a blackcurrant crossed with a gooseberry) – and blueberries surround the main soft fruit beds and are individually covered with heavy-duty nets draped over sheep hurdles to keep the birds off the developing fruit. Most of the berries are frozen for use during the winter, but the blueberries we eat straight from the bush. Of all the cultivated soft fruits, gooseberries and currants seem to freeze the best as whole fruit without losing their integrity. However, there are restrictions regarding growing blackcurrants and gooseberries in some states in the USA as they can attract pests and diseases that may devastate other crops, so do check local regulations before planting them.

ABOVE *In summer, pear tree boughs lie heavy with fruit and rely on wires for support. Beneath them each winter, partridges pick their way. We have yet to see one alight upon a bough.*

## PRUNING AND UPKEEP

The following certainly doesn't attempt to be a thorough treatise on the subject of pruning, but this is how we do it. Initially, one needs to decide whether to prune or not. A friend's father, on planting more than 100 varieties of fruit trees, consulted a local expert and was in turn asked how many apples and pears he intended to eat. The intention of pruning is to increase the volume (and quality) of fruit, but if each tree bore just one good fruit he would still have more than 100 fruits to eat. Perhaps wisely, he left the trees to 'free range' and still had a plentiful annual harvest.

Nick's father taught him to prune as a young boy on warm July evenings. The method was the one we now know as the 'modified Lorette system', which is suited to cooler climates. It involves cutting all mature laterals (shoots) from the main stem back to three leaves, and cutting sub-laterals (side shoots off the main laterals) to one leaf beyond the basal leaf cluster. Secondary growth after this pruning is

ABOVE LEFT AND ABOVE *The first blossoms herald the start of the growing season and, if we're lucky with no late frosts and good flying weather for the bees and other pollinating insects, soon the fruits are swelling. Honey bees are generally considered the principal pollinators of fruit trees so keeping bees on your smallholding should ensure the fruit sets. However, bees will travel up to 8km/5m to visit your trees so it is not essential for beekeeping to become part of your life if it doesn't appeal to you.*

OPPOSITE *Summer pruning is one of those jobs to be left for a warm evening when, at the end of the day, the task becomes a pleasure full of the scents of summer. The lush new growth can be sliced away satisfactorily and we pile the cuttings into the hand cart, wheeling it between the trees. As daylight fades and the hearth beckons (even on the warmest of nights), we have turned the shaggy clothed trees into neatly ordered, sculpted frames. As children, we called espaliers 'ghost trees' as they loomed out of the autumn mist with 'arms' outstretched.*

**THIS PAGE** *Bringing home the harvest marks the end of the growing year (and the start of the next), and we pile high the windfall apples as well as the carefully selected 'keepers'. Much of the former can be used for juicing and fruit leather, and the remainder will be gorged on by the pigs. The unblemished apples will be carefully stored for consumption over the coming weeks.*

JAMES DAY & SONS
NATIONAL MARK FRUIT GROWERS

JAMES DAY & SONS
NATIONAL MARK FRUIT GROWERS

cut back in autumn or over winter, when general shaping is undertaken. The principle is that winter pruning is to maintain a good structure and summer pruning is to encourage fruiting.

The soft fruits vary in their pruning demands, but autumn-fruiting raspberries are the easiest to manage. The plants fruit on new growth, so the whole top growth is cut back to just above ground level at the end of each fruiting season. Summer-fruiting varieties produce fruit on one-year -old canes, so in autumn cut back the canes that have borne fruit and tie in the strongest new blue-green canes to bear the crop the next summer.

Red and white currants are cut back in winter to an open cup shape with the principal stems reduced to a third of their length. Blackcurrants differ in that the majority of fruit comes from two-year-old growth, so you won't get a crop in the first year. The easy way to manage them is to plant them in threes and to cut back a third of your bushes to ground level after fruiting.

ABOVE *We lose a fair few apples and pears to wasps, which we trap in traditional glass bottle traps to minimize the risks to 'grazing' children. We have trained the girls to throw the rejects to the pigs on the other side of the hedge, and the sound of falling fruit now brings an immediate stampede. The children soon learned to test ripeness with a gentle twist of the stem, instead of biting into sour, unripe fruit.*

# THE
# ANIMALS

THIS PAGE *This year our lambs came from a friend's organic farm in Kent and are a Mule x Texel cross. The Mule bloodline makes them robust and hardy, while the Texel produces beautiful, succulent meat.*

# Keeping Livestock

*Introducing livestock is a step with many benefits, but with this comes responsibility and a commitment each and every day, at least for the lifespan of the animal. It is not to be taken lightly. However, creating a small home farm of 'just enough' animals to feed our family has been a thoroughly enjoyable if occasionally frustrating activity.*

**ABOVE** *In early autumn the pigs feast on fallen hazelnuts in the coppice, but they still welcome extra treats like windfall apples. When feeding, they also enjoy a good scratch and even pause mid-meal to roll over for a belly rub.*

**ABOVE RIGHT** *We keep little stock over winter. The geese will last into the first frosts, then head for the freezer marked 'Christmas', and only a few favoured hens will be kept for the following year.*

In practical terms, it can be easier to reach self-sufficiency in meat than in vegetables, and we have developed a system where a couple of pigs, a few lambs and a dozen or so birds, supplemented with wild game and fish from fishing trips, can support our family of four. The farmed animals have to be fattened over the spring and summer months for slaughter in the autumn, as once winter arrives the ground at Walnuts Farm becomes too wet for trotters, hooves and feet, and we retire to the fireside to enjoy the rewards of the growing season.

We choose our livestock on the basis of what animals are available locally, how easy they are to manage, and what will give us the best yields for the least amount of work. We have an agricultural store close to the homestead and local farmers and breeders advertize their

American turkeys have been a welcome addition because they roost in trees (so don't have to be put away at night) and are more or less self-sufficient. Our geese are the same, in that they free-range in the field and have been able to fend for themselves.

In terms of laying hens, we now select our breeds for their egg-laying performance. In the past, we have bought pure-breed hens at a premium price, but actually hybrid hens are more reliable in terms of the number of eggs they lay, and they carry on laying over a longer period. All our birds graze together in a mixed flock and new ones are introduced to the nesting box at night while the others are roosting on their perches. By morning, the flock have forgotten that they have an outsider in their midst and accept the new birds readily.

Our lambs are given to us as orphans (known as 'sock', 'bummer' or 'poddy' lambs) in early spring and raised over the spring and summer. This year's lot came from a friend's organic farm in nearby Kent. Our approach to keeping sheep is not to involve ourselves in wool-shearing or breeding – we're not full-time farmers, just homesteaders trying to produce enough food for our family and friends. Of all our stock, sheep are the most high maintenance so they are not the animals to begin with. Although we have developed a successful system by keeping them for just a few months to fatten over the summer, they are not as resilient or as low maintenance as our porcine and feathered friends.

available stock on a noticeboard. We like buying this way as the animals only travel very short distances, keeping their stress levels to a minimum, and we get to know their breeders.

We usually have an idea of the breeds that we are looking for. We have narrowed down our homestead pig of choice to those with Oxford Sandy and Black parentage. Our current weaner/feeder pigs are a OSB x Saddleback cross. These are both old breeds so are well suited to outdoor living and produce flavoursome meat. But the key to choosing a docile pig seems to be ear alignment. In our experience, floppy-eared pigs whose eyes are partially covered are quieter than prick-eared pigs like Tamworths.

The same desire for ease of management extends to our choice of poultry. Guinea fowl and North

# Bee Farming

*Bee farming goes hand in hand with a productive and fruitful kitchen garden, so a couple of years after we established the orchard and got the soft fruit cage up and running, we turned our attention to beekeeping. Our intention was not to be large-scale honey producers but to make 'just enough' honey for our purposes. Twelve 450g/16oz jars of honey is enough to keep us supplied throughout the year and we always have surplus to give away to family and friends.*

One of the great joys of beekeeping is opening up the hive on a warm day and hearing the contented hum of bees at work. The rich aroma of the wood smoker, mixed with the scent of honey, beeswax and cedarwood frames instills a sense of calm. And the quiet, methodical work of checking through each frame in the brood box to see that the queen is laying well is totally absorbing. The queen will determine the temperament of your hive, and if she is benign, her drones and workers will follow suit. Beekeeping has to be enjoyable and there is no pleasure in keeping an 'angry' colony – if so, the queen must be replaced, along with her courtiers.

The easy way to get started is to join a local beekeeping association. Over the winter months, when honeybees are hibernating, many

OPPOSITE AND ABOVE *Given benign bees, many keepers wear minimal protective clothing. However, the few stings one does receive can lead to an allergic reaction, so it's a case of 'better safe than sorry' and Bella uses a smoke generator to drift smoke inside the hive. The bees, suspecting a naturally occurring fire, gorge themselves on stored honey in anticipation of abandoning the hive and are unaware of the imminent human intrusion.*

associations run courses and talks to fill you in on the theory of beekeeping, but it is only by getting hands-on experience and paying a few visits to local apiaries that you get a feel for what's involved and gain confidence around these flying insects.

When we started out, we bought a second-hand WBC hive (designed by William Broughton Carr in 1890 and the classic UK beehive) from an local auction and our first honeybees were delivered in a cardboard box by a member of the local beekeeping association. We spread a white sheet over a ramp leading to the hive entrance and knocked the contents of the box onto the sheet. The bees marched up the ramp and into the hive, following the scent of their young queen. You can buy a queen and a nucleus colony from a good breeder, and a small colony on four or five frames will build up into a healthy sized colony of 60,000 bees by summer, when they'll be at their peak of honey production.

We now have three hives here at Walnuts Farm, two of which we bought in flatpack form. This seems to be the most economical way to buy a complete hive with all its working parts, including the roof, brood box, queen excluder, supers, frames and foundation wax. We also bought a fabulous old hive exterior at a farm auction, which we have now made watertight and draught-free.

The positioning of your hives is more important than you might think. Bees like a quiet, sheltered spot that enjoys the morning sun and is close to a water source. We got it wrong to start with, placing our first hive out in the field, where it was exposed to all weathers. The hives are now located in a sheltered spot in the kitchen garden, along the back fence and facing south but well out of the way of children and dogs. We can see the hives from our office, which comes in handy if we have an unexpected early spring swarm and need to dash out and catch the bees before they have upped and left.

ABOVE AND LEFT *The first check after winter is always something of a challenge as the bees block up any crannies or crevices with a sticky substance called propolis, and this can make the hive very tricky to open up and inspect. One beekeeper we know greases the frames with petroleum jelly before winter to keep the parts working and propolis-free.*

OPPOSITE *The role of the nursery bees is to keep the brood and larvae at a constant temperature and their pet hates include vibrations caused by strimmers, lawnmowers or a cack-handed beekeeper. Stillness and calm is all, so lifting the roof off the hive and extracting frames with the hive tool needs to be a smooth and deft operation.*

**THIS PAGE** *To harvest comb honey, lift the frame from the hive and gently brush off any bees (Bella uses a wing feather from one of our North American turkeys). It is then a brisk walk to the kitchen with the frames. Quickly close the door behind you – a few bees will want to follow, curious to know where their honey is going and keen to retrieve it.*

ABOVE *Thin rubber gloves protect the hands but still permit the gentle touch that is so critical when manoeuvring the frames. A specialist hive tool is used to lift the frames one by one for inspection. Bella assesses the health and vigour of the hive, looking for eggs and young brood, then removes new queen cells and adds extra frame space where necessary as part of a 'swarm management' plan. Handling the heavy filled frames, she also assesses the readiness of the stored honey for harvest.*

ABOVE RIGHT *Now relegated to a supporting role, thanks to a bee-sting allergy, Nick puts together frames in the workshop. His last sting, to an eyelid, turned his face the size of a pumpkin, and made public appearances daunting for both him and the public. Here, he remains both anonymous and secure in the dark workshop interior.*

Bee husbandry fits in with our homesteading way of life in that, like us, honey bees hunker down over the winter months, and the colony size is reduced to just the queen and a small nucleus of workers. When the weather is very cold, we insulate the roof of the hives with insulation board and 'heft' (or lift) the hives to check the weight and thus gauge the level of honey inside. In a harsh winter, we feed the bees with sugar fondant as there is little natural forage and they are reluctant to fly on wet, windy or cold days.

At the end of the winter, the surviving bees are hungry and bad-tempered after having been confined indoors. The first check in springtime is a challenge, as the bees seal up any gaps with a sticky resinous substance called propolis and this can make the hive difficult to open without jarring, which the bees hate. There is nothing more upsetting than opening the hive and seeing that your bees haven't survived the winter. Conversely, there is nothing more pleasing than watching the first few bees fly out of the hive on a warm, early spring day – a heart-warming sign that the new season is on its way.

Once spring has arrived, flowers like crocuses and viburnum start to appear and are an early source of pollen and nectar, as are trees like lime. Early forage is difficult to find for bees in rural areas and urban bees tend to fare better, plus city temperatures are usually a few degrees warmer. If you're lucky and it's warm early in the year, you may get a honey flow and even be able to harvest a few frames of honey in late spring. However, the traditional time of year for the honey harvest is late summer – we harvest in midsummer to allow more time to treat the hive for varroa mite (which all responsible beekeepers should do after the honey harvest, to avoid tainting the flavour of the crop).

After the harvest, we feed the bees with sugar solution to replace the honey we've harvested. The bees need time to extract the water and concentrate the sugars before temperatures drop. Come late autumn the hives are put to bed for the winter – empty frames are removed and put in the freezer to kill off wax moth, and the hive shrinks to a one-storey structure – just the brood box or chamber, where the queen and a small following reside. And so the cycle begins again.

# Harvesting cut comb honey

At Walnuts Farm, we produce cut comb honey as it's so simple and economical to harvest.
It's also the most unprocessed form of honey, as it's not extracted, heated or filtered.

Like any other crop, honey must be 'ripe' before it can be harvested, and that moment is reached when the bees have 'capped off' the comb on each frame with wax and the liquid honey is sealed in. The frames feel heavy when you lift them out of the hive. Brush off any lingering bees, then quickly carry the frame inside to work on it.

After several years of borrowing an extractor to spin the liquid honey out of its frame, we have now adopted a simpler approach whereby we cut the raw comb from the frame, then slice it up and place the blocks in glass jars. This method requires very little equipment and cleaning up afterwards.

First, we wash the glass jars (with rubber seals removed) then put them in the oven on a low heat (so the glass doesn't crack) for at least 20 minutes to dry them. We use a sharp knife to cut the honeycomb out of the frame. It comes away in one large slab and is then sliced into glistening chunks that fit through the neck of a sterilized jar. The lid is then sealed shut. The empty frame goes back in the hive for the worker bees to clean up any remaining wax and honey – nothing goes to waste.

If you want to produce cut comb honey, buy thin unwired foundation wax and tack it into each frame in the hive by early spring, so that the worker bees can start drawing out the flat sheets of wax into cells before laying down the honey stores.

Honey has great natural preservative properties and will store for a very long period. Over time, runny honey crystallizes into set honey and if you want to return it to its liquid form, sit the jar in a small amount of water in an ovenproof dish and gently warm it through.

# Poultry: Setting up a Flock

*After the long winter, the homestead comes back to life in springtime and the farming year begins in earnest. As early spring arrives and daylight hours increase, the hens resume normal service, laying an egg a day. The cockerel crows at first light and soon after, the automatic door of the henhouse cranks into action. The hens pile out and start scratching and pecking about, feeding on the fresh grass and insects that supplement their diet.*

In terms of choosing breeds, any young hen up to the age of two to three years old, with access to fresh grass, layers pellets, corn and some vegetable waste from the kitchen garden, will lay a beautiful egg with an orange-coloured yolk and thick white. Beyond that age, a hen's eggs will decrease in quality and number, while they increase in size and are sometimes misshapen.

We use a battery-powered electric net to keep our chickens contained in one area measuring about 150sqm/1600sqft. Both the netting and the henhouse are moved when the patch becomes bare due to the birds' methodical grazing. A galvanized metal pheasant feeder holds their food and is closed

**ABOVE LEFT** *We have a selection of water drinkers purchased from agricultural merchants and at farm auctions, but troughs and drinkers plumbed into mains water are also useful. All need to be kept ice-free if you keep stock over winter.*

**ABOVE CENTRE** *We have found electric netting to be the most effective, flexible method of fox-proofing our flock. It can be erected on a semi-permanent basis and*

kept taut between insulated straining posts, or used to corral the flock temporarily on fresh ground. A mower or chemical spray should be used to stop the grass below 'shorting' the fence.

**ABOVE RIGHT** *This large, sturdy pheasant feeder holds a 20kg/44lb bag of feed and won't blow over in the strongest of winds. The lid can be lowered overnight if vermin prove to be troublesome.*

**THIS PAGE** *An automatic door opener means your flock can be up feeding at dawn in summer while you remain in bed or get on with the many other tasks around the farm. At night the birds will put themselves to bed and the door closes after them. This works well for hens, but unruly ducks will sleep outside if you are not there to chase them to bed.*

LEFT *The space-saving ark design has overnight accommodation above a partially covered run, with nest boxes at waist height for convenient egg collecting. The handles at each end enable two people to walk it around the homestead, or wheels can be attached for single-handed operation. After a scrub to remove the lichen, this house could do with a coat of black bituminous paint, or we use our 'estate' grey to prolong its life.*

OPPOSITE *We have a selection of fixed and mobile poultry housing, and the latter is particularly useful in winter when we bring it and the few overwintering birds to the vegetable beds, where they are on 'gardening duty'. They will happily clear up the remains of harvested crops, keep the weeds down and manure the ground ready for the following spring sowing. The broody coop in front does duty out of season as quail housing.*

at night to deter vermin, and they drink from galvanized metal water fountains, which operate on a vacuum system and slowly release fresh water into the drinking tray.

During winter we move our portable chicken ark onto the kitchen garden beds, so the birds are within eyesight of the kitchen. The chickens scratch about on the vegetable beds and do some clearing and manure-spreading for us. They are the only livestock we keep over winter, and if we were hard-headed we wouldn't do this, as the hens have stopped laying and we have to buy feed to sustain them. There is a strong case for eating all the old stock at the end of the summer and buying in new, young point-of-lay birds early in springtime.

RIGHT *One nest box is sufficient for half a dozen birds and, if necessary, two birds will squeeze in together to lay their daily eggs. A nest of straw provides a soft landing and will not become mouldy, as hay would. At night internal shutters block access, to prevent droppings in the nest box.*

FAR RIGHT *A hat provides a handy receptacle for impromptu egg collecting. Eggshell colour is genetically determined and is unrelated to quality. We like a mix of colours for the boxes that we give away or sell.*

OPPOSITE *Getting the balance right between too few and too many hens is tricky. We find we really need only half a dozen laying birds, and even they will provide us with more eggs than we need in summer. But we almost always have more hens than this, partly to provide a few eggs in winter when we enjoy them more, and partly because we are growing up replacement stock. Of course, we cannot resist buying in a few birds from local suppliers and at poultry auctions as well.*

RIGHT *This house has lived a long life and at each stage grown taller. Here it is raised up on quarry tiles to keep its 'feet' dry, and with a sheet of 'wriggly' tin to provide a little shade.*

# Free-ranging Poultry

The free-range approach has its advantages in that the hens are less prone to pests and diseases as they have plenty of space, whereas permanent housing and wired chicken enclosures attract rats and other vermin. The disadvantages of free-ranging is that your hens are more vulnerable to predators, especially foxes. Long grass can cause the electric current in the fencing to short out, so we regularly strim around the fence perimeter to prevent this.

If kept in a permanent enclosure, hens will need access to grit, to enable them to grind up food in their gizzard, and they'll also need oyster shell as a source of calcium to make sure that their eggs have a hard shell. Neither of these supplements are required if you free-range your birds, as they will pick up grit and calcium as part of their daily routine.

We open the feeder later in the morning, to avoid having to feed the entire local wild bird population, and we close it in the evening when the hens go to bed, to deter rodents. Crows are persistent dawn raiders and we try to keep this 'daylight robbery' to a minimum. We find that shooting just one crow and hanging out the 'dead trophy' will act as a deterrent for several weeks – harsh, but effective.

The henhouse should be well ventilated but free of draughts, to prevent respiratory illnesses, and treated regularly with red mite powder to keep these itchy pests off the chickens. If the chickens don't want to go into their house at night, there's a good chance you've got red mite, because the birds don't want to be eaten alive and would rather take their chances outdoors.

Despite all this, we find the free-range approach less prone to problems, at least over the summer months, compared to the indoor equivalent.

BELOW *Vermin control is a necessary, but sometimes disagreeable, part of poultry keeping. Target practice is essential to ensure a humane shot, and this crow silhouette provides training for the beastly act. A silenced .22 air rifle is our preferred method. Anything else seems too noisy on a still, frosty morning.*

# Broody Hens and Hatching Out

An enjoyable way to increase your flock is to rear a few chicks of your own, but it will be at least six months (24 weeks) before they are fully grown hens laying eggs of their own.

The chances are that over the spring and summer months, one of your hens will go 'broody', which means that she'll start sitting on a clutch of eggs in the nest box all day long and return to the box as soon as you've thrown her out. If you don't have a cockerel, none of these eggs will be fertile, but if you do and you want to raise chicks, transfer the broody hen to a separate house or 'broody ark' with the eggs, so she can sit in peace for the 21 days until they hatch.

We have always had more success hatching out chicks with a 'broody' than with an incubator. The broody hen will sit on the eggs to keep them warm and turn them regularly. Once the chicks have hatched out, she will keep them warm and protect them. You won't need to set up an infrared heat lamp or house the chicks indoors in a vermin-proof enclosure. You'll just have to supply them with a shallow (to avoid drowning) bowl of water and chick crumbs – a small-sized, high-nutrition feed. The hen will also teach the young birds how to act amongst a mixed flock. Incubator-reared hens have few of these social skills and have to learn them fast.

Another advantage is that you can use a broody to hatch out other species of bird. We've hatched Aylesbury duck eggs using a hen as a surrogate mother. You can buy fertile eggs by post and this is a cost-effective way to introduce new species to your flock. Our Cuckoo Marans have all made very good mothers, while Bantams are renowned for their great mothering skills so they are worth keeping for this reason alone. A favourite broody-inclined bird (marked with a coloured anklet so you will always know her) is certainly worth the effort and expense of keeping her over winter.

If hatching by incubator, the eggs should first be marked with a pencil with the date that they were collected. They remain viable for several days, but the sooner you incubate them the higher the hatching success rate. The more sophisticated, and therefore more expensive, incubator mechanisms will maintain a constant temperature and turn the eggs periodically over the 21-day period. Humidity is also important to prevent the eggs from drying out and the outer shell sticking to the embryo.

It is always thrilling when you hear your first chirrup coming from the incubator, but do not be tempted to help the chick out of the shell. Let it happen naturally, even though it might look like a bit of a struggle. The other chicks will follow in succession over the next two or three days.

# Designing a Henhouse

We started out with a good-quality second-hand henhouse and over the years it's been repaired several times over. The first house was bought via an advertisement in the local pet shop window and was thoroughly scrubbed inside with disinfectant to remove any traces of red mite and painted grey – our estate colour. It housed our first flock of six ordinary brown hens.

THIS PAGE *This ancient and now rickety house exhibits many of the attributes of our perfect henhouse. It is raised above ground level, which prevents rising damp and avoids vermin making a home beneath, as well as offering shelter from both sun and rain. The hens naturally seem to wish to 'go up' to roost.*

ABOVE LEFT *Sketched elevations and three-dimensional drawings of the proposed henhouse aid the decision-making process. We take inspiration for our build from the new porch on which we sit, helping to tie the henhouse design to that of the house.*

ABOVE CENTRE *Oak posts left over from our porch build are 'over engineered' for our needs, but will result in a henhouse to last. Four solid posts from ground to eaves will provide structural integrity, and raise the house to a level where it is easy for us to manage daily tasks.*

ABOVE RIGHT *Clay peg tiles utilize readily available materials and, with painted boarding, ensure a substantial and warm interior. Ventilation can be provided at ridge height, and the tiles and boarding can be removed for deep cleaning. Crucially, each part is replaceable as and when necessary.*

It's probably wise to find out whether you enjoy keeping hens before you invest in new housing. Originally, our henhouse was on the ground and we added a tin sheet shelter as hens dislike getting their feathers wet in the rain. We then added legs to get the house off the ground and to stop the wooden structure from rotting prematurely.

Next, we put it on stilts so it would be at the right height when we cleaned it out without having to stoop and so that the hens could shelter beneath it. In time, we've replaced the wooden floor and the wooden roof with corrugated tin. Both materials have advantages and disadvantages. Wood is warm and well insulated and you can repair it easily, but it does harbour red mite in its nooks and crannies and is virtually impossible to deep clean if you have a red mite infestation. Tin gets hot in summer and cold in winter but it keeps rain out, is cheap to buy, lightweight to transport and doesn't rot.

If we were building our perfect henhouse from scratch, we'd build a rather grand structure for fun, using some of the oak posts left over from the building of our porch. The house would be raised, to provide shelter beneath for the birds and to facilitate egg collecting at waist height. It would be inspired by a fisherman's net-drying shed, with shiplap or feather-edge boards painted grey or with black bitumen. We would give it a beautiful pitched roof of reclaimed clay tiles, with perches inside that were higher than the nest boxes. In many henhouse designs, nest boxes are installed at a higher level than the perches so the birds want to roost in them at night, which makes them mucky for egg laying.

In an ideal world, our dream henhouse structure would stand on sandstone staddle stones to deter rodents, or even on a sturdy iron-wheeled chassis, allowing us to move the house around the plot with ease. It would look beautiful.

# Keeping Other Birds

*Apart from egg-laying hens, there is a whole world of poultry out there to suit the homesteader. We have had great fun and delicious meals from our attempts at rearing hens for the table, but also notably ducks, guinea fowl, geese and turkeys. Amongst our favourites is the humble quail.*

As well as providing good meat, quail are worth keeping for their delicious creamy eggs, which our children almost prefer to hen eggs. Soft-boil them for a couple of minutes in a pan of boiling water and they are ready to serve. Quail are prolific layers, leaving beautiful mottled brown eggs in shallow dips in the ground each day. We like to blow the eggs and use the shells to decorate the home (see Decorating with Natural Finds on pages 196–197).

We've always enjoyed keeping guinea fowl for their meat, feathers and occasional eggs, when we can find them. Guinea fowl are secretive layers and hide their off-white eggs in long grass. They roost in trees so need little management, but some people dislike them as they can be noisy. We like the fact that they raise the alarm when danger is present and alert the rest of our less vigilant poultry flock. Guinea fowl meat is lean and very similar in taste to chicken. It is delicious roasted or panfried. The spotted grey and white feathers have a natural beauty and we have mounted a few in frames to hang on the wall.

Other meat birds we raise include Aylesbury duck and turkey, but duck is our most successful discovery. It is dark in colour and delicious pan-fried in thick slices and served on a bed of fresh salad leaves. The soft, downy feathers make beautiful natural fillings for pillows and cushions too.

OPPOSITE *A general-purpose poultry house raised on stone blocks can house a variety of poultry, being flexible enough to accommodate a changing flock. One year it might hold a laying flock roosting inside on perches; the next summer, with the perches removed, it could contain growing table birds. With a shallow-angled ramp, geese and ducks will be able to waddle up at night.*

RIGHT *'Wild' turkeys (as opposed to their heavy, domesticated cousins) and guinea fowl will roost out in your trees whatever the weather, but they will also benefit from a dry, open barn with beams to perch upon during wet weather. Just don't park your tractor or car beneath!*

BELOW LEFT *Free-range guinea fowl meat is at the gamey end of the 'chicken-flavour spectrum' and is much easier to produce than chicken. The birds are self-sufficient to a great extent, once they are mature enough to fend for themselves, being almost fox- and dog-proof.*

BELOW RIGHT *We don't like to see good material go to waste, especially when it comes from one of our animals, and this feather down from our Aylesbury ducklings will fill a good-sized pillow.*

OPPOSITE *With heads down feeding, the pigs are oblivious to Bella restocking their ark with straw, but on other occasions take a keen interest in its interior and get terribly excited by the introduction of a new bale.*

BELOW *We feed excess garden produce straight to the pigs and they tuck in gratefully, so not even these blown lettuces go to waste. Pigs can be picky – sweet, young beets are preferred to woody, old ones, and turn*

*their mouths bright pink as they messily devour them.*

RIGHT *Feed time is a good opportunity to accustom the pigs to our presence. Daily handling stops them from going wild, which is important when loading them into a trailer at the end of summer. 'Slap, scratch, despatch' is the approved management technique.*

FAR RIGHT *A curly tail is a sign of good health, but it's the last thing you'll see if your fence is not sturdy.*

# Keeping Pigs

*We have been keeping pigs for the past six years now. We buy a couple of weaner or feeder pigs (8-week-old pigs) in early spring and rear them outdoors throughout the summer months, during which they supplement their concentrated feed with nettles and brambles and clear the land for cultivation. In autumn, when they reach a weight of approximately 80–90kg (176–198lb), we send them off to the local slaughterhouse so that the freezer is full of bacon, sausages, pork chops and hams for the winter months ahead.*

The beauty of this seasonal way of rearing pigs is that the ground does not get too churned up. We don't have to buy in large quantities of pig feed to maintain the pigs' body weight over the winter months. And we avoid complex animal husbandry issues that go hand-in-hand with pig breeding and farrowing.

As soon as the ground hardens at the end of winter, our weaner pigs arrive. We move the pig

ark to a new site and fill it with fresh straw to make a comfortable bed for the new arrivals. Each year we devote an area of about 20 x 50m (65 x 165ft) to the pigpen. We also move the water supply and the electric fencing posts and wire. We start off each new pen with three strands of electric wire, one of them running very close to the ground, so that the piglets can't shimmy underneath.

This year, we situated the pigpen in a scrubby patch of woodland just beyond the kitchen garden so the pigs could clear the brambles and ground cover. Woodland is a pig's natural habitat and the dappled shade cast by the trees is ideal, as direct sunlight can cause sunburn. The pigs' strong snouts and muscular necks make them perfect soil Rotavators, and since we started keeping pigs six years ago, they have cleared large swathes of brambles that were encroaching on the perimeter of our two-and-a-half acre field.

We knew nothing about pigs before we came here, so we enrolled on an introductory course in pig-keeping. There are only a few requirements to ensure happy, healthy pigs. Their housing should be sited on dry, draught-free ground, as pigs don't like damp conditions. They need a plentiful supply of fresh water as they drink several litres/pints a day. To supplement their diet, we feed them grower nuts morning and night as well as any waste green matter from the kitchen garden. Windfall apples, pears, plums and other overripe fruit also go down very well.

Pigs are surprisingly low maintenance – easier than chickens in some ways, as pigs have no natural predators and don't have to be put to bed at night. They are also very resilient. We have to deal with paperwork that goes with identifying and moving pigs on and off your land, but this can be done online, so check for local regulations. The only other essential is electric fencing, which they quickly learn to respect, to keep them where you want. Alternatively, sturdy stock fencing will do the job if you want to create a permanent secure area, especially if you have roads nearby or are bordered by neighbours.

OPPOSITE ABOVE *Our pigs provide entertainment both in life and on the plate. We had one that escaped and took three hours to catch, and another that escaped only to find and drink a can of beer. It promptly fell asleep.*

OPPOSITE BELOW *Our pig ark has a galvanized steel roof and no floor (straw is thrown onto bare earth). At the end of the season the ark is moved and the straw burnt.*

ABOVE *Pigs can be very amusing. They have a docile temperament and, like dogs, enjoy a good scratch on the rump or a tickle behind the ears. They are sociable animals and like company.*

BELOW LEFT AND RIGHT *We never ate very much pork before we kept our own pigs, but the quality and flavour of our own meat is nothing like we've ever tasted before. It's sweet and full of character, so unlike the bland-tasting pale meat of indoor-reared animals.*

# Hand-raising Orphan Lambs

*We started keeping sheep three years ago, as organic lamb is expensive to buy. When they are slaughtered in the autumn, the cuts we order from the butcher include rack of lamb, chops, ground mince, kidneys and boned shoulder and leg of lamb, and the sweetness and tenderness of the meat is indescribable. We've found that four small sheep can comfortably feed a family of four and our friends throughout the year.*

The cycle starts in spring, when the three-day-old orphan lambs are delivered. These are the lambs that a ewe is unable to suckle – she only has two teats, so anything more than twins is not sustainable. Bottle-feeding lambs is time-consuming, so most commercially-minded farmers are happy to give up orphans rather than see them go to waste.

Raising these lambs is sheep-keeping in its easiest form, as there is no breeding or shearing involved. At first they are bottle-fed powdered milk, then weaned onto a compound pelleted feed (lamb creep) and grass. The nutritional value of the grass is at its highest in spring and early summer. When this starts to decline, the lambs need hay and a concentrate feed and things start to get expensive.

For the first few weeks, the lambs are kept in our potting shed on a bed of straw and only venture outside on warm spring days into a small area of grass enclosed with wooden hurdles. We shut them back in at night, out of reach of predators like foxes and crows. Once they are big enough to fend for themselves, the sheep are turned out into the field, but having been bottle-fed they always come rushing to the gate at the sight of us.

Sheep kept for only a few months are low maintenance. They need a regular supply of fresh water and we supplement the nutrition they get from grass with a bucket of feed mornings and evenings, but this is more as a treat than for any other reason. They are also sprayed with a chemical treatment to prevent flystrike and biting lice.

OPPOSITE *The arrival of the orphan lambs coincides perfectly with the school Easter holidays, providing daily entertainment for the children and their friends. There is nothing more life-affirming than having a soft little lamb, with wrinkly, ill-fitting skin that's too big for it, sitting on your lap, greedily feeding on its lukewarm bottle of milk. Where we live in Sussex, orphan lambs are known as sock lambs, probably because they were wrapped in socks in the farmhouse kitchen to keep them warm.*

BELOW LEFT *The milk replacement powder available from our local agricultural merchant arrives in a bag with making-up instructions usefully printed on the back. Four bottles will fit into a wire rack so, if necessary, all four lambs can be fed simultaneously.*

BELOW RIGHT *Once weaned, the lambs move on to grass and concentrate 'creep' feed. The sock lambs are always the smallest of their siblings and need to take every opportunity to put on weight over the summer.*

LEFT *Condition scoring the sheep is an art that requires experience and practice, and as we keep only four sheep this experience is not attainable without getting our hands on other sheep too. Many smallholder groups run courses on condition scoring to teach the method and to enable those with just a few sheep to keep their hand in.*

BELOW *Our lambs arrive already ear-tagged with individual and flock marks from their holding of origin. These tags stay with them throughout their lives. As with the pigs, movements of sheep between holdings need to be recorded officially, and the relevant authorities informed of each movement using the correct form. The required paperwork is not daunting, and is there to ensure traceability of both the animal throughout its life and the final meat product.*

# Fattening the Sheep

In autumn, we bring the sheep into the wildflower meadow at the front of the house and we love being able to watch them graze the long grass against the backdrop of our small farmhouse. This only takes place once the flowers and grasses have set seed, to ensure a good crop of wildflowers the following year.

The sheep do a wonderful job of keeping the meadow down. Without them we would have to scythe the meadow and rake it off, in order to keep the soil nutrition level depleted to encourage wildflower growth and discourage the competitive grasses. The sheep graze it tight and reduce grasses that compete with the flowers.

This wild meadow grazing marks the end of the sheep-keeping year and the next job is to condition score them – the method of assessing the body condition and proportion of fat to meat on the animal before they go off to slaughter. This is really difficult to do, as their woollen fleece makes the sheep look big enough to eat. Experienced sheep farmers use their fingertips to determine the amount of muscle and fat covering the vertebrae, loin, dock (tail root) and ribs. In addition, we weigh them to make sure, aiming for a target weight of just over 40kg/88lb to yield a carcass half that weight.

We then enclose the sheep in hurdles and they are collected in a trailer and taken 10 minutes up the road to our local slaughterhouse. From there, the carcasses are taken to the butcher and hung for a few days before coming back to us cut, all packaged and ready to eat.

THIS PAGE *Our little meadow was perhaps created originally as a 'nursery' field where stock could be watched from the house during lambing or illness. In the 1940s it was used to rear caged rabbits for food, but more recently had been cut as a lawn. It has now returned to a more productive (and pretty) state.*

# THE
# LAND

OPPOSITE *A wild meadow has to be managed carefully, and its subtle beauty lies in the fact that over the course of the seasons and year it evolves and changes.*

BELOW *Common knapweed (Centaurea nigra) has colonized much of the meadow and in some years becomes almost too dominant. The lambs, however, enjoy nipping off the flower heads and graze on the tasty morsels first.*

RIGHT *We were given a pocketful of yellow rattle (Rhinanthus minor) seeds by a passing walker and the seeds have quickly established themselves in the front meadow.*

FAR RIGHT *Snake's head fritillaries (Fritillaria meleagris) have been introduced for a little early colour and brighten the meadow in the spring light.*

# The Wildflower Meadow

*When we first moved here in May 2005, the land had been left uncultivated for many years and the field was a mix of tall grasses, like meadow foxtail and plantains, together with common sorrel, buttercups, common spotted orchids and red clover. We wanted to encourage this natural tapestry and the wildlife it supported.*

As well as maintaining the existing meadow, we decided that we would turn the front garden into a wildflower meadow. We had a romantic notion of mowing a path to the front door through a carpet of wildflowers and billowing grasses, and thought this strategy would be low maintenance. We soon discovered, however, that the more help you give to the temperamental wildflower species, the more easily they will colonize areas. The annual wildflower yellow rattle (*Rhinanthus minor*) has been our secret weapon, as it is semi-parasitic on perennial rye grass and prevents it becoming dominant.

We tried planting ox-eye daisies (*Leucanthemum vulgare*) and cornflowers (*Centaurea cyanus*) in the

ABOVE *A wild meadow has to be managed carefully and its subtle beauty lies in the fact that over the course of the seasons and year it evolves and changes.*

meadow, painstakingly gathering the seeds in the late summer and growing them in plug trays to transplant into the front meadow. But wildflowers have a will of their own, and many of the introduced species disappeared, then reappeared in different areas. It's rather like starting a painting: you have an idea of how you want it to look, but it never turns out quite as you imagined.

We have sown a specially created bee mix around the beehives. This is a blend of perennials and annuals that provides nectar and pollen to honeybees. We sowed the mix in early May, pressing it firmly into the ground, then watering it in well. It has proved very successful and flowers beautifully into autumn. If you want instant colour and something less subtle than a native wildflower meadow, a purpose-made mix is very effective.

OPPOSITE ABOVE LEFT
*In summer, ox-eye daisies cut a swathe through the meadow margin. These distinctive flowers are typical of wild meadows but invariably will have been 'encouraged' when seen in profusion. We shake a few dry seeds into the soil pushed up by moles in late summer, then tread them in.*

OPPOSITE ABOVE RIGHT
*The vibrant colours of the bee garden and the bees' specially planted meadow contrast with the 'wild' equivalent, even if that too is managed rather than truly wild. Here, a mix of annuals and perennials chosen for their long flowering season spill over the path.*

OPPOSITE BELOW
LEFT *Camassia, a North American native, has been planted wherever the bulbs seem to benefit from, or at least endure, our damp clay soil. Flowering in early spring, camassias hold on just long enough for the buttercups to join them. Typically, spring flowers start with the white and blue varieties then move on to hot yellow and red plants as the temperatures slowly increase and the days get longer.*

OPPOSITE BELOW RIGHT
*Poppies and cornflowers blend with the encroaching bracken and almost obscure a white beehive.*

## MANAGING THE MEADOW

We've tried different approaches to managing the wildflower meadow, but the basic principle remains the same: to impoverish the soil and reduce competition from grass species.

For the first few years, we cut the long meadow grass with a strimmer in late summer, once the grasses had grown up and the wildflowers had set seed. We raked it off with a hay rake to remove nutrients and finally cut the grass as tight as we could with the mower. Then we planted bulbs such as the North American native *Camassia quamash* and fritillaries (*Fritillaria meleagris*) to up the flower count in spring. Planting out these bulbs has proved more successful than transplanting seed plugs, as they have now started to spread and colonize more areas of the meadow by slower seed dispersal.

Since we have started keeping sheep, we have used them to assist with meadow management. We bring them into the front meadow in late summer, once the wildflowers have had a chance to set seed, and they graze it down. No need now to strim, rake and mow. However, we do have to keep the sheep away from the hedges and the roses close to the house, which they seem to prefer to grass!

ABOVE *Our lurcher hunts moles (and is surprisingly successful, given their subterranean habit) as the meadow grass is rowed up and raked off. Letting an established lawn 'grow out' into a meadow can be a very successful enterprise, as the constant mowing over a period of years will have impoverished the soil already.*

OPPOSITE *Our favourite common spotted orchid (Dactylorhiza fuchsii) grows well here at Walnuts Farm and each year we count up the first flower spikes, trying to predict whether it will be a good or indifferent year for them. Invariably, some years favour one particular species or another, or the seasons shift a week or so either way to surprise us.*

OPPOSITE *On the Sussex Weald, we are fortunate to enjoy a show of bluebells growing among the ancient deciduous woodlands each spring. They grow in such profusion here that we are in danger of taking them for granted, but the sight of a woodland floor enveloped in a hazy blue carpet delights us all.*

ABOVE *In spring, the first pale green shoots of the hornbeam hedges and trees surrounding the house are eagerly anticipated.*

RIGHT *The presence of gorse (*Ulex europaeus*) among the hedgerows betrays the origins of the fields around as open heathland.*

# Establishing a Woodland

*The beauty of choosing to plant a woodland is that you can choose the species mix yourself, but make sure your chosen stock will thrive on your land. When the young trees are first planted, you will need to guard against rabbits and deer and control brambles and other weeds until the trees become established.*

The species mix you choose should be a reflection of the local tree cover and your site conditions. We chose a native mix, including birch (*Betula*), rowan (*Sorbus*), hazel (*Corylus*), Scots pine (*Pinus sylvestris*), goat willow (*Salix caprea*) and the shrub dog rose (*Rosa canina*), as well as oak (*Quercus*) and hornbeam (*Carpinus betulus*). We planted the trees according to variations in ground and soil over small areas. Thus the goat willow, which loves damp conditions, went into the floodplain area, for example, while the Scots pine and the sturdy hornbeam predominate on the dry sandy banks above.

## PLANTING YOUNG TREES

Notch planting bare-rooted young tree seedlings or 'whips' is a pleasant way
to spend a crisp winter day, hopefully with the sun on your back. Use a sharp-
edged spade to make two vertical cuts into the soil, connected at right angles.
Pull back and then push forward on the shaft with one hand as the spade sits in
the second cut, and into the space behind the spade head drop the roots of your
tree whip. Spin the whip to splay the roots, and remove the spade. The whip
should sit upright at the apex of the two cuts and at the same depth as grown in
the nursery. Firm in with a heel, tug to ensure the whip is secure, and move on
to the next. Follow up with tree guards, as required.

In summer you will need to water young trees regularly, using a mobile water
tank or pumping water to the site, You will also need to combat weeds, as grasses
and other vegetation will compete for the water your young tree needs if it is
to survive. Mulch mats are squares of fabric or fibre that fit around the base of
newly planted trees to prevent weeds from growing and can either be purchased
or of your own devising. We considered making them ourselves from corrugated
cardboard, but instead we sprayed a solution of the systemic herbicide glyphosate
around each stem to create a 1sqm/10sqft bare-earth chemical screen.

ABOVE LEFT *Tubular
deer guards protect the
vulnerable young trees.
Within one summer, some
of the Scots pines surprised
us by vigorously growing
up, and out to the light.*

ABOVE RIGHT *We weren't
sure about planting oaks as
they grow like weeds here,
self-seeding all over the
homestead or sprouting
from acorns buried by
squirrels. Either way, plenty
of young 'sports' pop up
each year, and it's easy to
guard the ones we would
like to see mature.*

**THIS PAGE** *Establishing a woodland can be as easy as simply deciding to stop mowing or topping a piece of land, or preventing animals from grazing there. Look for natural regeneration from seed stock already present or blown in from the locality, and guard against rabbits and deer if necessary. Here, we've planted additional hazel and rowan trees amid existing oaks and hornbeams*

# The Nuttery

*On our homestead, we inherited the remnants of a nuttery. A small number of hazel trees had been coppiced over a period of years for hazel rods and nuts. We have continued the process, cutting down the largest poles to ground level and using them for firewood, while awaiting the regrowth for use in fencing.*

Our mixed-age coppiced woodland produces sweet green hazelnuts in late summer and early autumn, and there is something of a race between us and the squirrels to get to them first. Any nuts that fall to the ground are eagerly gobbled up by the pigs, who we keep in the woodland in autumn using two or three strands of electric fencing.

If you are growing trees solely for nuts and want a plentiful harvest, you will not be coppicing but pruning to encourage fruit production on a network of easily reached stems. The two tree styles look very different, but the nuts will taste the same either way.

We also grow a few coppiced sweet chestnuts. Keep the squirrels off them and they will keep you in roasted chestnuts all winter, attract the deer in autumn (in case you wish to harvest them too), and provide strong rot-resistant poles for fencing with wire, or as the uprights in a woven hazel fence.

OPPOSITE *We don't know who originally named Walnuts Farm. It may have been a marketing name to sell a tenancy, or just a fashionable conceit, but when we moved here walnut trees were nowhere to be seen. We have added a couple to the nuttery, but it will be some years before we are eating our own green hulled walnuts.*

ABOVE LEFT *Sweet chestnuts are an easy find for a child, and in autumn our girls come back from the woods bearing pocketfuls of them for roasting in the embers*

of the fire. We make sure we always have a few at Christmas to cook with Brussels sprouts, as well as for making stuffing.

ABOVE CENTRE AND RIGHT *Our coppiced hazel trees produce nuts in late summer, and it's a contest between us and the squirrels as to who gets to them first. Hazelnuts are far more delicious when fresh and green than in their dried state. We box trap the squirrels and eat them too, so the nuts they eat are not really wasted.*

# The Front Garden

*Although most of our land is given over to food or fuel production, we do have an area of garden on the south side of the house that we use for entertaining and eating outdoors. We refer to it affectionately as the 'pub garden' because it is just two squares of gravel edged by box/boxwood hedging to echo the double-fronted symmetry of our small farmhouse.*

ABOVE LEFT AND RIGHT *'Kew Gardens' is an English rose bred by David Austin. This one has survived our voracious sheep. In spring, primroses sprout at the base of the woven hazel fence.*

RIGHT *The box hedging grows thick and lush here, fed from below by wet subsoil. Gravel paths ensure feet stay dry even after rain, and this space can be enjoyed (with coats on, if necessary) all year round.*

On one side we have our well-weathered table and chairs and a large umbrella, whose canvas has faded to a pretty shade of pale terracotta. Into the gravel we have thrown handfuls of hollyhock seeds, which have grown well in these dry, gravel-garden conditions; we're particularly fond of the really dark, almost black ones.

The hedging took four years to get established. Bella will never forget the blisteringly hot August day that it was planted, and leaning out of the bedroom window to shout instructions to Nick and her mother while newborn baby Peggy slept soundly. But not everything has turned out quite how we imagined. Along the rusty iron railing, bought second-hand at auction, we planned a row of cream rose bushes interspersed with lavender. However, our first flock of sheep quickly put an end to that idea by chewing off the tops of the roses, and although lavender grows well in the gravel in front of our outbuilding, it has never liked it here, no matter how much grit we add to the clay subsoil.

# The Courtyard

*On balmy summer evenings, we like to eat outside with friends and family in the sheltered courtyard space that lies between the house and the outbuildings.*

We light beeswax candles in the lanterns that hang on either side of the pigeon-grey door to the workshop and carry the kitchen table out of the back door into the courtyard, followed by a selection of benches, stools and chairs. To mark the occasion, we dress the table in a favourite old French linen tablecloth and bring out plates in soft shades of pink, grey and khaki. The dusky pink hollyhocks that self-seed and grow freely in this patch of gravel are picked and arranged informally in a pitcher on the table. Their pinky hues look wonderful set against the warm red brick of the outbuilding.

Other additions to the table include an old glass wasp trap, more beeswax candles – we love their warm scent of honey and they never smoke and rarely drip – a storm lantern and our 1960s stainless-steel pistol grip knives and forks.

Our antique wine glasses are as old as the house and have been slowly accumulated over the years. In summer, our tipple of choice is chilled rosé, preferably from our friend's organic vineyard. A typical dinner menu might include home-smoked trout (see pages 122-123) on rye bread with a squeeze of lemon juice and freshly ground black pepper as a starter, followed by crayfish from the brook (see pages 104-105) with home-made mayonnaise, to keep the pink theme going!

OPPOSITE *On summer evenings, dusk falls late and we like to enjoy every last moment of the light. The east-facing brick wall of the outbuilding radiates the heat of the day and is a perfect spot for the wisteria we have trained along it as well as for the* Lavandula 'Hidcote' *that grows in the gravel. As the light fades and the bats begin to fly, we light the candle lanterns on either side of the outbuilding door so we can linger outside a little longer.*

ABOVE *Wasp traps are a requisite for lunch parties outside. A sticky sweet jam or cordial seems to be the most successful lure, even though wasps, like hornets, are carnivorous.*

RIGHT *Beeswax candles may be expensive to buy but they are worth every penny, as they give a clean burn, rarely drip or smoke, and last for hours. In the past, bees were kept as a valuable source of wax for candles as well as for honey, but even though Bella uses beeswax to make furniture polish and beauty balms, she has yet to try candlemaking.*

OPPOSITE *We were early adopters of the now fashionable 'glamping' ethos and are the happy owners of a beautiful white canvas bell tent, which can sleep up to six people quite comfortably. It is very low-tech and incredibly simple to put up and down. There are no bendy plastic poles or nylon to contend with, just pegs, string and a central pole, and adults can stand up inside it rather than crawling about on*

*all fours. Now, 14 years on, it is still going strong and very popular with the children and their friends.*

LEFT *Well-seasoned lamb burgers are one of our favourite alfresco meals.*

BELOW *Nick hangs our heavy cast-iron Dutch oven from an ingenious wooden hook that can be hoisted up and down over the fire, depending on whether you need more or less heat.*

# The Brook

*At the beginning of the summer, we set up a summer camp on a piece of land that drops down to the brook and is sheltered by several large ash trees and a horse chestnut. Early in the year, this area is a carpet of snowdrops and primroses, then it changes and evolves with the seasons. The focal point of the camp is a circle of old oak tree stumps rolled into position around a fire pit we've created.*

During the long summer evenings, we hang a cast-iron Dutch oven from a tripod made from three sturdy hazel poles that support the heavy, lidded pot, and enjoy some simple one-pot cooking using both seasonal and foraged produce. Nick lights the fire well in advance, so the cooking can be done slowly and evenly over roasting-hot embers rather than leaping flames.

We also enjoy feasting on the crayfish that populate the brook. Our girls, Peggy and Flora, caught their first crayfish using forked sticks to pin them down and shrimping nets to scoop them up, and later progressed to night-time forays with a torch spotlighting them in the shallow water.

# Catching and cooking crayfish from the stream

Native to North America, Red Signal crayfish (*Pacifastacus leniusculus*) are an introduced species here in the UK and require removal to protect the indigenous species that they are displacing. Trapping crayfish requires a licence from the Environment Agency, which is issued free of charge but which prescribes the type and size of trap used in order to minimize the chance of catching other species.

Where present, crayfish are easy to catch over the summer months using traps baited with meat or even bread. If you are preparing for a midsummer feast, you must either put out plenty of traps or utilize a perforated storage barrel sunk into flowing water in which to collect your catch and keep them fresh and alive until you have enough. Alternatively, a few crayfish will keep in an empty bucket under a damp cloth in the cool shade of an outhouse for a day or so until needed.

We cook the crayfish in our cast-iron Dutch oven suspended from a tripod over an open fire. Four minutes at a good rolling boil is plenty. The crayfish go in a dirty black–brown colour and come out a resplendent crimson. The change is fantastically theatrical – seemingly a magical transformation when witnessed for the first time.

Cool the crayfish immediately in fresh, cold water to prevent them from overcooking. We like to eat them with generously buttered hunks of fresh bread or dipped in home-made mayonnaise – it's a deliciously messy business.

OPPOSITE *We use wild garlic, or ramsons, to make a delicious garlic mayonnaise to accompany fat chips.*

ABOVE *Most of the boletus species of mushrooms make good edibles and they are one of the easiest species to identify as they have pores rather than gills, a bun-shaped cap and a bulbous stem. This* Boletus edulis *is a prize specimen. If you are an amateur when it comes to identifying mushrooms, go hunting with an expert forager.*

RIGHT *One of the great pleasures of foraging is it that it gives a walk a great sense of purpose and puts you in touch with the seasons.*

# Foraging

*The pleasure of collecting free food from the hedgerows and surrounding land appeals to the hunter-gatherer within all of us. After ten years on the homestead, we know where the best mushrooms will appear, where to forage for sloes and where the juiciest blackberries can be found. It is a joy to be able to harvest this natural forage at just the right moment, before birds or other wildlife get there first.*

Early May is the start of the foraging season here at Walnuts Farm. At this time of year, we head down to the shady cool of the brook and are overwhelmed by the pungent scent of garlic in the air. Wild garlic (*Allium ursinum*), with its large spear-shaped green leaves and delicate white flowers, is also known as ramsons. It is a wonderful source of flavour, imparting garlicky juices from the leaves and flower stalks at least three months before our kitchen garden crop of garlic has come to maturity.

# Making sloe gin

The easiest time to spot blackthorn (on which sloes grow) is in springtime, when from a distance the heavy blossom can look like a late fall of snow on the hedgerows. Make a mental note of the location and return in autumn to harvest the sloes. Our hedgerows frequently produce bumper crops and we fill our pockets with the hard berries when out checking the sheep or walking with the dogs.

Sloes look rather like grapes or blueberries, but when picked fresh they are a challenge to eat – tart and sour. Once they have been 'blet' or bruised and allowed to partially decompose, they become sweeter and rather more palatable.

The sloes we forage end up in the cellar in a large glass jar with additional sugar and a bottle of the cheaper kind of gin. We like to use less sugar than most recipes suggest as we're not keen on a sweet 'medicinal' taste, and like to keep some of the original astringency of the fruit.

**1kg/2¼lb sloes**

**500g/2¼ cups granulated white sugar**

**1 litre/35fl oz gin**

Freeze the sloes overnight and then defrost them (so their skins burst), or prick each one with a fork.

Sterilize an airtight bottle and pour in the frozen (or pricked) fruit. Now pour in the sugar. Top up with the gin. Seal the bottle and upend it a few times to mix everything up. Store the bottle somewhere cool and dark. Turn the bottle every other day for a week, then once a week for two months. Open, strain into sterilized storage bottles and enjoy!

Another favourite early in the year is elderflower, which is only available for about a month from late May. It grows like a weed here and we pick it in great quantities. See overleaf for our recipe for elderflower cordial.

Later in the year, in early September, we forage for ripe blackberries and sloes, which both freeze well until needed. At this time of year, there are also wild mushrooms to be found, which we add to risotto, one of our favourite autumn dishes.

LEFT *Lined up on the table in the library ready for a taste test are three different sloe-based drinks and an almost empty bottle of elderflower vodka. The sloe vodka, gin and brandy have been made by us and local friends, who often join us for a tasting to compare their qualities.*

OPPOSITE *In early summer, the brambles produce flowers full of nectar that provide wild forage for Bella's bees. Each year, the pigs are given the job of rooting up this prolific plant, but we still manage to harvest a great crop of blackberries to freeze for smoothies, crumbles and blackberry whisky.*

# Making elderflower cordial

Elderflower cordial is the taste of the British summer, with its subtle floral notes and refreshing taste. We love it, and for all the years that we've been making it, we never seem to produce quite enough to see us through the year.

Elders grow like weeds in our hedgerows. The flowering season is short and the flowers are at their best only for a month from May to June, depending on the weather. The frothy white flowers are best picked early in the day, so as soon as they have been warmed by the morning sun we are out gathering them. There are many recipes for elderflower cordial, but ours is loosely based on Sarah Raven's recipe and is as follows:

1.35kg/6¾ cups granulated white sugar

the flowers from 15–20 elderflower heads

2 oranges, thinly sliced

2 lemons, thinly sliced

30g/1oz tartaric acid (in powdered form – buy from a pharmacy or online)

*MAKES two 750ml/26fl oz bottles*

Measure out just over a litre/quart of water and pour it into a heavy-based saucepan. Add the granulated sugar and stir it with a wooden spoon over a low heat until it dissolves, to prevent the sugar from burning.

Once the sugar has dissolved, turn up the heat and bring the solution to a rolling boil. Drop in the flower heads and return to a boil. Take the pan off the heat.

Place the sliced fruit in a large mixing bowl. Sprinkle over the tartaric acid powder. Pour in the hot sugar syrup with the flowers. Cover with a clean tea towel/dishtowel and leave to steep for at least 24 hours.

Next day, strain the cool liquid through a piece of fine muslin to remove any bits and pour the cloudy liquid into sterilized bottles. It will keep in the fridge like this for a couple of months, but ours never seems to last that long!

# THE
# WORK AREAS

# A Hard-working Barn

*On a busy homestead, a barn serves many purposes. We need somewhere to store hay and straw and to provide a multi-purpose space for many different activities during the year.*

**BELOW AND OPPOSITE BELOW LEFT** *A tractor stands outside the barn at our friends' farm on the Isle of Oxney. Modern baling equipment produces rolled bales (opposite below) that can only be handled by heavy machinery, and a barn must be large to hold them. There are still small balers available for the homesteader with limited storage space.*

**OPPOSITE BELOW CENTRE AND RIGHT** *When using materials in a minimalistic manner, the quality of the fixings, joints and overall proportions take on extra importance and deserve careful consideration. Here, simple, utilitarian materials, including galvanized steel and treated softwood cladding, create a pleasing effect. Account must be taken of the wind load on big and heavy doors when they are open and the hinges must be robust. The recessed doorway of this barn provides shelter for workers as they enter and protection for the interior and its contents.*

RIGHT *In an ideal world, any homestead would be equipped with numerous flexible and adaptable outbuildings of all kinds, but this is rarely the case. In the absence of the perfect array of buildings, the homesteader may have to build his or her own. In the design of this modern barn, the wider landscape has been considered and the steel uprights of the portal-framed barn echo the steel uprights of the vine support poles.*

The barn must be accessible from the house and yard, yet should not impact negatively upon the house or garden. Aesthetics are as important as convenience. Living in an historic environment, it is easy to assume that a pastiche, or a rebuild of an existing barn brought in from another site, may be an appropriate choice, but a modern interpretation could be equally fitting.

We particularly like our friends' new barns on the Isle of Oxney in Kent, where they have combined simple utilitarian materials and an agri-industrial aesthetic. The materials used are comparatively inexpensive and blend well with existing structures. The galvanized hinges are not oversized for visual effect – the great barn doors require strong support.

A simple structure of a tin roof on a pole frame – an open-sided or 'Dutch' barn – will keep the weather off and can be built from reclaimed telegraph poles or, more beautifully, be of oak-framed construction. The roof could either be reclaimed or made of new corrugated galvanized zinc or profiled powder-coated steel sheeting. An open-sided structure allows air to circulate and offers ease of access, but part of the barn may be boarded for security or additional weatherproofing.

A barn is not only a place of storage and temporary animal or equipment housing, but also a dry space for working on all manner of projects, so a typical concrete screed floor is a practical choice. Old barns had floors of beaten earth with sections boarded over for threshing grain. If all that is needed is dry storage and the soil is light and free-draining, you may be able to avoid concrete flooring. Alternatively, a few tons of road stone can form a permeable hard standing for vehicular access and create a rough-and-ready floor that will satisfy many purposes.

# The Woodyard

*Our house is solely heated by wood, which feeds the Rayburn range cooker in the kitchen and the wood-burners elsewhere, and we get through around seven to ten tons or more of wood each year. Cutting and preparing the seasoned wood takes place in the woodyard, which has semi-permanent walls of corded wood offering shelter from the wind.*

Cutting and preparing all that seasoned wood might be seen as quite a chore, and if you're of this opinion then there are always local woodcutters who will deliver at a reasonable rate. However, cutting your own firewood can be satisfying, and after a taxing day in the home office, splitting logs is a fine way to take out one's frustrations with the world. On a cold day the exercise will warm you up, too, and more cheaply than any gym membership.

Every winter we have a few trees to harvest. We cut the wood into roughly 1.2m/4ft lengths and stack it in cords measuring 1.2–2.5m/4–8ft to dry out during the summer months. The following winter we saw the wood to the desired length, split it where necessary and stack it on the porch, just outside the kitchen door. We can fit a couple of tons there and having it so close to hand allows us to reload the log baskets without even having to put our boots on.

The pleasure of cutting your own wood is that you get to know the different wood types, how they handle under the saw and the axe, the different drying rates, and how they burn. Ash is a favourite here, as we have plenty of overgrown coppice at the height of its maturity. There is no regret in harvesting these beautiful fully grown trees – when cut cleanly, they will regrow from the stump in the following summer and will be ready to harvest again for firewood in 15 years or so, the whole process being repeatable over generations and indeed centuries.

ABOVE LEFT AND RIGHT *A stack of wood from an overgrown hedge that we coppiced lies drying out under sheets of corrugated iron. These must be secured against the wind, as they can be quite lethal if allowed to blow around the yard. The big butts cut into rings will be split into pieces to fit the fireplaces.*

OPPOSITE *The pleasing rhythm of lift and drop, using the axe's own weight and momentum to chop more efficiently, quickly becomes addictive. Nick bends the knees on impact and wears steel-toed boots to avoid injury.*

On more than one occasion we've driven home to find the track blocked by a windblown ash and these are quickly devoured by the chainsaw. The timber is high in dry matter and will burn unseasoned when necessary. Ash is our 'emergency' tree – when, by poor planning or continuous bad weather, we have run low on seasoned supplies, we cut an ash to keep us going. Its clean white timber cleaves beautifully and is a pleasure to split.

A lot of the firewood sold near us is sweet chestnut, which is prone to spit and crack. It's fine in a woodburner but potentially hazardous in an open fire. We are keen on the much-maligned sycamore – it dries in just a few short months over summer and splits easily under the axe. Oak is not our favourite for the fire, where it seems wasted. It also takes at least two or three years to season and is heavy to handle, but we like the sawdust for smoking fish and meat. Holly trees make a great fire, as do hawthorn, but beware the spikes. Willow and alder we cut aplenty, but mainly just because we have lots of both, for the benefits in heat output seem negligible compared to the labour spent.

All this chopping produces plenty of big chips of wood that can be used as kindling and the saw work results in great piles of wood chippings, which can easily be swept up for animal bedding or mulching the fruit cage paths. The finer chips created in the workshop from hand-sawn hardwoods or by the chainsaw can be collected to be used in the smoker.

OPPOSITE *A neat stack of logs on the porch always draws admiring comments from passers-by. The appeal seems to be universal. We think of it rather like a full freezer, or cash in the bank. We've 'banked' the wood and it will keep us going over the coming months.*

BELOW LEFT *A 'saw horse' holds the poles to be sawn, and its dimensions match the length of our fireplaces so we can use it as a guide to cut perfectly sized logs.*

BELOW AND BOTTOM *Smaller branches can take a lot of effort to collect and cut and it is tempting to leave them where they fall, but they do provide good kindling or fuel for charcoal making. As for the wood chippings thrown up by the saw, they are a useful resource not to be wasted.*

# Making charcoal

Nick was given a small home-made charcoal maker as a birthday present by Bella's mother and it has proved to be a practical gift. When tidying up the remnants of a hedge trim, it is easy to set up the charcoal maker with its contents of seasoned hardwood branches within the centre of the bonfire. Once the fire has subsided, another sackload of lumpwood charcoal is ready for use.

We used to buy locally made woodland charcoal to cook over, as lumpwood charcoals have the advantage over commercially available ones in that they are chemical-free, have no additives and don't taint the flavour of food. Also, they are easy to light and burn evenly, producing enough heat to cook lamb burgers to perfection.

Charcoal making goes hand in hand with other woodland management tasks, such as clearing and coppicing, which take place on the homestead in the autumn and winter months. There is nothing more evocative and delicious than the aroma of woodsmoke from a bonfire, and this is when we take the opportunity to make charcoal. Seasoned hardwood sticks are heated inside a steel cylinder at the centre of the bonfire to a high temperature in a low-oxygen environment.

To make charcoal, you need well-seasoned dry wood, preferably a hardwood like oak or ash. We load the small steel cylinder with 12–14 sticks cut to length so that they'll fit inside, packing them together tightly. Fit the steel lid securely to keep the air out and place the burner in the middle of the bonfire or, better still, build the bonfire around it.

When the fire is spent and the canister has cooled down, usually about 24 hours later, it is ready to open. Do not attempt this too early, or your charcoal sticks will ignite on contact with air and be reduced to ash. On opening the charcoal maker, you will see that the sticks have been converted to lumps of black charcoal, ready for the barbecue.

# Using a smoker

While out cutting firewood in the woodyard it makes sense to set up a secondary task, and tending to a smoker seems to fit in well. The smoldering oak sawdust in the grate needs frequent checking to ensure it stays lit, but there is plenty of time to get on with other tasks too.

At the start of the trout-fishing season in March or April, Nick will come home with a bag filled with glistening rainbow trout. We gut and eat the smaller ones, very simply pan-fried in butter, but the larger trout – 900g/2lbs and upwards in weight – are smoked. We fillet them into two beautiful pink sides of fish that are then threaded onto wooden skewers. The skewers are woven horizontally through the flesh to create a structured frame so that the trout doesn't fall apart during the cooking process.

When smoking fresh fish, we use sawdust or woodchips from hardwoods to fuel the smoker, as softwoods contain resins and give a harsh, acrid taste to the smoke. Also, smaller particles like sawdust and woodchips burn more evenly. The most difficult part of the process is lighting the sawdust. We use matches and a blow stick to get it going before closing the fuel drawer. You'll need only two or three handfuls of sawdust for a couple of hours of smoke.

Before the fish is placed in the smoker, it must be cured with dry salt, then washed under cold water and patted dry. The salting helps the smoke 'stick' to the surface of the fish and adds depth of flavour. Hot smoking both flavours and cooks the fish and is so called because the heat source is close to the product being smoked. The slow cooking process prevents the fish from drying out and, despite the name, the temperature should not exceed 50–80°C/122–194°F.

# The Porch

*Our porch measures 5 x 1.5m/16 x 5ft and has been a welcome addition to our homestead. The backdrop for many different activities, it is truly a multi-functional space, allowing us to work outdoors while sheltered from the weather.*

The porch was the first addition made to the house in 100 years. Originally, we commissioned a skilled local craftsman to build a green-oak frame with a clay-tiled roof to make a dry wood store just outside the kitchen door, but it is now so much more than that. We soon realized that if we decked it with wide oak boards we could step out onto the porch in socks or bare feet at any time of day. Throughout the summer months, we leave the kitchen door wide open and the dogs hang out there, watching the world go by. We plait garlic and onions in this space, hang out our home-made chorizo sausages to dry in the airy rafters and stack logs here, not to mention storing many pairs of rubber boots, storm lanterns, fishing nets, rods and walking sticks in the eaves.

LEFT *The porch offers a transitional space between indoors and out, and is so useful that we wonder how we ever managed without it. The green-oak posts sit firm on sandstone blocks that were quarried locally and were originally part of a long-abandoned farm building. We dug them out of a muckheap when we moved here and stored them for just such a project.*

RIGHT *On a stout beam above the back door sit boots in every size to suit the unprepared visitor, plus everything else that we want to keep dry and close to hand but don't want cluttering up the boot room. The pegs pinning the oak joints have been left long in places to act as coat hooks or a place to hang a dog lead.*

# Making chorizo sausages

Salting then air-drying pork is a delicious way of preserving and maturing the meat. Although we've eaten salamis and chorizos from all over southern Europe and beyond, we never realized how simple they were to make and how well they dry in our damper British climate. Unlike air-drying a whole leg of ham, which takes many months of dry weather, chorizo sausages only take 8-12 weeks before they are 'ripe', firm and hard to the touch, and ready to eat. We add plenty of garlic, smoked paprika and freshly ground black pepper to the mix, as we like them really spicy.

1.25kg/2¾lb minced/ground pork (we ask our butcher to prepare a 'salami mix', which is 10 per cent fat mince/ground meat from just under the skin and 90 per cent lean mince from the shoulder and front legs)

5 tsp/25g table salt (2-2½ per cent of salt by weight)

2 tbsp hot smoked paprika

4 cloves garlic, peeled and crushed

freshly ground black pepper

½ tsp acidophilus powder (a natural enzyme that will help the salami to develop the correct mould) or a mature chorizo with a natural white bloom on the skin

beef middle casings soaked in large bowl warm water for 20 minutes

*MAKES 6 chorizo sausages*

Mix the meat and salt together thoroughly in a large bowl. Add the smoked paprika and mix well. Peel and crush the garlic into the mix. Finally, season with black pepper.

Feed the rehydrated casing onto the spout of a funnel and knot the other end of the casing. Fill the funnel with salami mix and push it through the funnel into the casing to form a sausage shape. Squeeze the casing to fill the case evenly and prevent air pockets forming.

When you've created a 25cm/10in length of sausage, cut and tie the top. Thread with garden or kitchen string and hang in a cool, well-ventilated place. We suspend ours from the high rafters of the porch, close to the house and safely out of reach of any vermin. The natural casing enables the chorizo to dry out naturally and slowly, while acting as a barrier against flies and airborne bacteria.

We hang a ripe chorizo, which has already developed its natural white bloom, amongst the fresh ones, to help the sausages develop the correct mould. Alternatively, you can add ½ teaspoon of acidophilus powder (a natural enzyme) to your meat mix, to help the salami develop the correct mould. This is available from health food stores or your local pharmacy.

# Making a willow wreath

We planted a screen of willow trees at the bottom of our field for two reasons: firstly, to hide an ugly drainage pipe that crosses our land, and secondly, to provide a fast-growing crop of willow poles to make repairs to the willow fencing that encloses the kitchen garden. A happy by-product of this crop are the bendy green willow whips that, when green in summer, can be manipulated into wreaths. The children make small versions to decorate the chicken house, outbuildings and the doors of all four bedrooms. By Christmas, the wreaths are no longer green but brown and dry, and we push fruiting ivy, red rosehips and any other berries we can find into the loose weave. The fresh material doesn't wilt if we give it a daily mist with a water spray.

**six lengths of green willow,**
  **approximately 1.5m/5ft long**

**secateurs/pruning shears**

*MAKES a wreath about 30cm/12in*
  *diameter*

Take one length of green willow in your left hand. Form a rough circle and hold it in place while you wind in the tail end. Start weaving in the next length and then the next, working in and out of the frame as you go until you have a circular structure. Use secateurs to trim off any ends. Hang the wreaths up until ready for use.

# Braiding/plaiting garlic

Garlic needs a long, eight-month growing season, from November through to July, to give the bulbs time to separate, swell and mature, ready for harvest. When the leaves turn yellow in midsummer, we know it is time to lift the bulbs out of the ground, preferably on a warm, dry day. We leave them lying on the warm soil for a few more days, then carry them to the porch on drying racks, leaves and all. It's important to keep the long yellow leaves intact, as they are the 'strings' you need to weave the garlic into a good, strong braid.

Our garlic braids may not be as tight and professional-looking as those you see for sale on the market stalls in France, but we delight in the fact that we have grown our own and that this crop will keep us in garlic for the year to come. In theory, all the bulbs should be a similar size, but home-grown ones aren't always that uniform. We just tie them all together into the braid as they come.

**20-30 garlic bulbs, with long dried-out leaves still attached**

**string or garden twine**

*MAKES one garlic braid, about 60cm/2ft in length*

When we are ready to start braiding, we carry our kitchen bench out onto the porch, as its long, narrow shape lends itself to the activity perfectly.

As if you were braiding hair, start with three garlic bulbs on long strings and braid them together. Each time you turn a string over the next, add in a new bulb. Keep the braid tight so that the bulbs hold together well and don't fall out when you hang it up.

When your braid has reached 60cm/2ft in length, tie the leaf tops together in a knot, attach a loop of string and hang the finished braid from a hook in the kitchen or store.

# The Workshop

*As so much of our time is spent there, we consider the workshop to be very much part of our living space as well as a working space. Thus it is equipped with a fireplace for warmth on cold days, chairs of various styles and in various states of repair, and a radio to keep us informed of what's going on in the outer world.*

Above the fireplace we have accumulated a selection of interesting finds from the garden and elsewhere: a flint from a school expedition; skulls from fly-caught pike and a fearsome-looking one that turns out, on closer inspection, to be from a humble rabbit; a thermometer and barometer; trophy feathers from various 'kills'; signage and stencils. Surrounding these are tools and useful kit of all kinds. On either side of the workshop are long benches, one equipped with a vice for serious endeavours, such as sharpening the chainsaws, and the other under the window for more artistic pursuits, including potting out seedlings during cold spring days and sorting and storing produce during warm autumn ones.

The floor of brick paviors laid on bare earth shows all the signs of previous use and has been worn thin at the thresholds by generations of human feet. In one corner of the workshop is a favourite feature – a beautifully constructed brick depression. It is the perfect shape for workshop debris to be swept into and then collected up, the depression perfectly fitting the standard shovel heads still manufactured today.

OPPOSITE ABOVE AND BELOW *A farmer Nick worked for when he was a student used to say that 'a job is not finished until the tools are put away', and we try to follow his rule. It helps to have a designated place for everything, and with wall and ceiling space utilized, tools are available to hand and any absence is noticed. There is, of course, always the temptation to deposit heavy or bulky items just inside the doorway when rushing to complete some other task, but all too soon the doorway would become blocked.*

RIGHT *When digging around the homestead, we have unearthed various interesting finds that simply cannot be thrown away and these, together with other curiosities and decorative finds, now congregate above the workshop fireplace.*

BELOW *Under the window runs a long workbench made from a single wide plank. This is a quiet place for potting out seedlings, painting, mending or undertaking other tasks that require daylight as well as a roof over the head.*

Many winter days find one of us at the vice, sharpening one of our chainsaws between logging sessions. While initially this seems an interruption to the task in hand, it quickly takes on its own rhythm. On goes the radio and out come the socket spanner, bristle brush and files. The jaws of the vice are wound out and the saw is clamped firmly in place by the chain guide bar. Then commences the task of filing a new cutting edge to each tooth in turn, seeing it take on a gleaming silver, in contrast to the old resin-blackened ones, as the slither of metal is shaved off. While this activity is going on, we often become absorbed in a programme on the radio and are reluctant to finish!

The workshop is the place for all those little repair tasks that require just five minutes of free time or are awaiting the ordering of a spare part, and these can be accumulated until a rainy day arrives and the backlog can be cleared. It is also a great resource, being stuffed with useful materials of all kinds. Offcuts of oak planking are neatly stacked beside oak posts and beams that await a building project, sections of copper piping stand in the corner and rolls of lead sheeting are shelved above. It is a place for glues of all kinds and string of all lengths.

The key to an efficient workshop is that everything must have its place, if only to prevent the collection of tools, bicycles and equipment that is stored within it from being deposited just inside the door by every other member of the homesteading team.

ABOVE *Grease guns, chain strainers and spare saw chains are kept safely out of the way, hanging from a board at hand height.*

OPPOSITE ABOVE *We painted the ceiling and joists white to reflect daylight in to the dark side of the workshop. Off-duty poultry water fountains overwinter here, and a ladder is hung from pegs set into the wall.*

OPPOSITE LEFT *At quiet times Nick can amuse himself with some little project or other, one day fashioning farm animals for the children from offcuts of ply or aluminium sheeting, on another re-engineering a galvanized feed scoop as a lampshade.*

OPPOSITE RIGHT *Pigeonholes that have migrated from a solicitor's office now serve as below-bench storage for boxes of chisels and plumbing sundries, foot pumps, generator parts and a spool of strimmer line.*

# The Store

*Having a cool, dry, dark room in which to store the season's potatoes, apples, pears, onions, shallots and garlic is incredibly useful. And there is something reassuring about being able to squirrel away your harvest and come back to it later in the year, particularly during the winter months when little is growing outdoors. Our storeroom sits at the back of the workshop but is divided from the main space by a single door, so it is always cool and dark inside.*

We don't grow large varieties of maincrop potatoes as these types of potatoes are relatively inexpensive to buy from farm shops or even the supermarket. Instead, we focus our efforts on tasty little varieties such as Pink Fir Apple. These have a delicious nutty taste and texture that's hard to match. Although we eat most of our crop freshly dug from the ground, when we have a bumper harvest we leave the potatoes to dry out a little on the soil/dirt, give them a quick brush and put them in hessian sacks or wooden trays to store. They will keep well for several months in cool, dark conditions.

Onions and garlic store well too and, unlike potatoes, they don't need to be kept in the dark. We store shallots and red and white onions loose in wooden apple trays in the store. These stack neatly on top of one another so take up very little floor space. Shallots and the yellow sturon type of onions seem to keep best, while red onions turn soft quicker, so we try to use them up first. We start most of the dishes we cook with an onion and a few garlic cloves and it's so useful to be able to nip out of the back door and grab a few from the store.

RIGHT *We bought our crates at an agricultural auction in Kent and they've proved invaluable. They are stamped with James Day & Sons National Mark Fruit Growers and we like knowing their provenance.*

OPPOSITE *Our vintage galvanized roll-top metal feed bin sits in the storeroom. It is the ideal way to keep feed dry and mould-free, and it keeps the rodents out. The bin was given to us by a friend and it belonged to his father, so probably dates back to the 1950s. It is beautifully engineered, sitting on casters so you can wheel it about. Morning and evening we open it up and dish out feed from the open sacks before heading out to the animals. Pig food is stored in the compartment on the right, and sheep and chicken food on the left. It will comfortably hold four large 20kg/44lb sacks.*

# Storing pears

Pears are quite an underrated fruit, but in many ways they are far more interesting in flavour and texture than apples. We grow two varieties – Beurre Hardy and Doyenné du Comice – and the pear trees form a decorative espalier down the central avenue in the kitchen garden.

Beurre Hardy are picked in August when they are hard and are ready to eat in about three weeks. Doyenné du Comice are harvested in late September to October and are best picked when they are slightly underripe, to prevent bruising. This variety of pear will keep until Christmas. To check whether your pears are ready to harvest, give the stem a gentle twist. If the fruit comes away easily from its twig, it is ready; if not, leave it for another few days. Remember, the fruit won't ripen all at the same time, so you'll need to make several trips.

Once picked, handle pears very gently to prevent damage and don't let their skins touch. We carefully wrap each pear in newspaper and store them in a wooden crate in the storeroom. Pears wrapped in this way and kept in cool conditions last longer. We bring them inside to ripen for a couple of days before eating.

THE
HOUSE

# The History of our Homestead

*Walnuts Farm is sited in a quiet backwater of the Sussex High Weald in England's southeastern corner. Our homestead is likely to have been inhabited since the 1500s, which ties in with the date attributed to the oak-framed barn adjacent to the farmhouse, which is a building of special architectural interest due to its age. The farmhouse itself dates from around 1800–1825 and is built on the site of an older house. It retains the principal inglenook fireplaces and cellar of the previous house and many of its beams and timbers were recycled from the older dwelling.*

BELOW *The farmhouse has two large inglenook fireplaces in the kitchen and sitting room. Both have a large 'bressummer' beam made of oak – a hardwood that has always been in plentiful supply in this part of the country. Although originally an open hearth for cooking, the chimney was lined and a solid-fuel Rayburn installed in the 1970s, for cooking and heating the house. We burn well-seasoned wood rather than coal, as wood is a much 'cleaner', greener burn.*

We suspect the house itself would have always been on a smallholding of around 30 or 40 acres, sustaining an extended family who perhaps sold surplus crops when possible. Locally, poultry production for the London table market was popular once the railways arrived, and during the Second World War a thriving rabbit enterprise was established here in the front meadow. More recently, dairy and then beef cattle were farmed here, but are sadly no longer commercially viable.

The great fireplace that still exists at the western end of the house was no doubt added to a medieval Wealden hall house in a spirit of modernization, doing away with a central hearth and creating a new dedicated kitchen area in the process. The late Georgian rebuild retained this fireplace and placed it within an almost symmetrical double-fronted little house that was then the height of modernity, but now is very much of the type imagined by nostalgic dolls'-house makers, or dreamed of by city workers in idle moments between spreadsheets.

The house was rebuilt with just two south-facing rooms downstairs divided by a central staircase, leading to two bedroom chambers above. What was once an exterior door led down from the rear via brick steps – now worn smooth – to a stone-lined cellar.

The ground-floor rooms at the rear became the new kitchen, dairy and meat-processing room. A previous inhabitant remembers, rather gruesomely, 'the floors

ABOVE RIGHT *This little brick outbuilding is an early extension of the kitchen and houses the bread oven. Our neighbouring property was once a mill house and our bread oven is unusually large for a domestic dwelling, so perhaps it was used to bake bread on a commercial scale for the local community?*

ABOVE *The painted dovecote is our addition to the house, but traditionally many farmhouses would have had one to raise squabs (young pigeons) for fresh meat. Ours has never housed doves, only pied wagtails and, once, crows, who seemed to like nesting high up and undisturbed in the pop holes.*

running with blood when livestock was butchered'. We have continued in a similar vein, and the hooks lining the central beam are still well used when we are jointing venison or making sausages.

Our homestead has clearly always been a hard-working house and was designed to be such, with the more formal rooms to the south-facing front accessed from the front door, and the cool north-facing rooms for work accessed from the track (and now the kitchen garden) opening onto a small courtyard with an outbuilding opposite.

Within the fireplace in the 'new' kitchen is a brick bread oven large enough to bake a dozen loaves. On the northern exterior wall, jutting out about 3.5m/12ft from the ground, is a braced hook-ended beam. It is placed at a good working height that suggests cattle may have been hung there for butchery or a large pig for slaughtering. Although we've not tried that, it certainly has proved useful when skinning and jointing fallow deer, much to the intrigue of passing walkers on the footpath.

Walnuts Farm has always been a commercial building and it has worked hard for us too. It protects us, shelters us and, with the surrounding fields and woodland, also feeds us, as well as providing an income, such that we are excused the burden of commuting to the city to make our livings.

BELOW LEFT *Heavy-duty iron hooks line the central beam that runs the whole length of the kitchen. They have proved invaluable when jointing venison carcasses and hanging home-made chorizo sausages to dry out. Perhaps they have always been used thus.*

BELOW CENTRE *The brick hearth in the sitting room is well worn and pitted with age. Originally, the fire would have been laid directly on top of it but a wood-burning stove is now in place, as is an iron grille to improve the flow of air. The woven log basket was made by a local underwoodsman to our design. It is a large, deep rectangle that holds a huge quantity of logs to feed the fire throughout the evening.*

BELOW RIGHT *During cold spells, stacks of well-seasoned logs fill every recess in the kitchen as the house fires need constant feeding – they are our only source of warmth, as we do not have modern central heating. On damp days, the logs are brought in from the porch for a final drying out beside the Rayburn.*

OPPOSITE *The south façade of the farmhouse is late Georgian. It is a pleasingly symmetrical double-fronted house with a lead porch and fine brickwork with a decorative pattern of glazed grey headers. These attractive grey bricks were first created by accident rather than design, when old brick kilns had hot spots that would cause the clay to vitrify and darken. We painted the the window and door frames in 'Pigeon' by Farrow & Ball.*

THIS PAGE *The east end of the kitchen is home to our long refectory table. This came with us from our previous home, a tiny cottage where it filled the whole kitchen. Here, 14 people can sit down together for lunch or supper. We sand the table down and whitewash the surface from time to time to keep it looking respectable.*

# The Homestead Kitchen

*Our farm kitchen sits on the north side of the house, which is traditionally the coolest place for storing and preparing food. It is the 'hub' of the homestead and where most of our indoor activities take place. A new kitchen can be a big investment, but ours has evolved as a loose arrangement of unfitted cupboards and pieces of furniture. We wanted it to be atmospheric; a place for the family to live in, do homework, draw and read, as well as cook and prepare food.*

It can be dark in here on a summer's day, so the first thing we did when we moved here was to paint all the wood panelling and the brickwork a creamy buttermilk shade to bounce the light around. Most of our kitchen furniture was bought at auction or from local antique shops. We like simple, utilitarian pieces. The long, white-painted kitchen table measures 90 x 250cm/3 x 8ft and is our main work station. It is the perfect height for kneading bread and preparing food.

ABOVE *Our Rayburn range cooker is built into an inglenook fireplace and its two-tone 'sable' livery betrays its 1970s origin. Filled with seasoned logs from the woods and hedgerows, it provides heat and hot water for the house, as well as a hot plate and oven.*

FAR LEFT *The white brick ledge above the Rayburn is home to an idiosyncratic collection of treasures, including Nick's collection of pewter drinking mugs (filled with turkey, pheasant and guinea fowl feathers).*

LEFT *Fresh eggs are best kept at room temperature rather than in the fridge. Ours are stored in an old wire basket on the kitchen windowsill.*

ABOVE *The white unit made up of six square cupboards was used by Nick's father to hold his office papers when he was a London solicitor. Nowadays, painted white and with a slab of limestone on top, it is a store cupboard for dried goods. Unfortunately, our whippet has learnt to lift the door latches with his nose and it is not uncommon to come down in the morning to find him tucking into a packet of dried noodles!*

OPPOSITE *Although a light, bright and pleasing space to work in, the layout of the kitchen is not particularly ergonomic as we find ourselves walking the whole length of the room to put things away.*

As soon as we started planning the kitchen, we realized that in order to have a connection with the produce we grow, we needed to be able to step straight out into the kitchen garden. Until then, there was only a window on the east side of the house and to get to the garden we had to walk out of the door at the other end of the kitchen and around the back of the house. As luck would have it, we found a pair of old French doors that fitted the existing window recess exactly.

Once the doors were in place, we hung long, pale grey linen curtains on either side – not very practical but they look good. A large coir mat acts as a barrier to mud and a shelf to the left of the door keeps dirty boots and clogs out of view.

## BAKING BREAD

Simple pleasures are some of the finest. But that simplicity does not mean that they are without refinement or depth. Good bread falls into this category, and a slice of home-made bread is something to savour. With just a smearing of salted artisan butter, it makes the finest of meals.

We keep to a regular routine of bread making and find that a loaf made every other day is more than adequate. In the refrigerator we store our 'starter' dough, originally gifted to us by a Californian bread-fanatic friend, and which we have kept alive for several years now. The starter contains natural yeasts from the air captured in a floury environment and is kept alive by periodic refreshments of water and flour. It gives off a wonderful ripe, yeasty aroma that adds to the sensual pleasure of bread making.

Using a wooden spoon, we combine bread flour, salt and the starter dough in Nick's mother's mixing bowl, then knead gently. We leave the dough to rise on the Rayburn, covered with a damp cloth, while we head off to other tasks. Inevitably we arrive back at the kitchen with less-than-perfect timing, but the dough is generally kind to us and allows us to 'knock it back'. It retains enough energy to rise again, this time formed into a ball and placed in a straw hat (our version of the baker's proving basket).

Once risen a second time, we tip it onto a baking tray and place in the oven to bake. The results vary, depending upon our diligence, the consistency of the dough and even the atmospheric conditions. But whether perfectly risen with air holes to rival a Swiss cheese, or of a more 'biscuity' shape and texture, the results never fail to stand head and shoulders above the commercial bagged equivalent.

## A quick sourdough starter

This is an easy sourdough starter that cheats a little to get the starter going, rather than waiting to capture naturally occurring yeasts from the environment.

15g/1 tablespoon active dried yeast
200g/1½ cups strong white bread flour
50g/½ cup rye flour
300ml/1¼ cups warm water
*MAKES 250g/9oz*

Add the dried yeast to the strong white bread flour and rye flour. Mix with the warm water, and leave for at least 24 hours in a warm (but not hot) place to develop.

## Making sourdough

Our favourite sourdough recipe comes from Alison Walker at *Country Living* magazine.

300g/2¼ cups strong white bread flour
75g/¾ cup rye flour
1 teaspoon salt
250g/9oz starter mix
200ml/¾ cup warm water
*MAKES 1 loaf*

Mix all the ingredients together in a bowl until a sticky and ragged dough forms. Either gently knead on a board or continue with the spoon in the bowl until the dough is smooth, elastic and bouncy. Leave in a lightly oiled bowl to rise for about 2 hours. Knock back and leave to rise for another 10 minutes. Shape into a round and place in a proving basket for 1½ hours.

Preheat the oven to 220ºC/425ºF/Gas 7. Turn the dough onto a baking sheet and slash the top with a very sharp knife to break the surface and allow an even rise. Bake in the preheated oven for about 1 hour, or until the loaf sounds hollow when tapped on the base. You will get to know your oven and preferred timing after baking a loaf or two. While you're waiting, replenish the starter with flour and water and return it to the refrigerator for next time.

## COOKING FOR THE FREEZER

We freeze a lot of fresh produce, including lamb, pork, poultry and even honey, and we also try to do as much batch cooking as possible to make things easier when we come in from outside and don't want to start to cook dinner from scratch.

Home-made lasagne is always popular, but a surprise success story with the younger members of the family is wild game bird casserole, which seems to improve in flavour with freezing. Label and date any dishes made for the freezer – it's surprising how quickly one forgets what one's made and when.

# Game bird casserole

Here at Walnuts Farm young pheasants are easy pickings in the autumn, when they are young and naïve. Some of the pluckier birds even wander up to the house, lured by the grain feeder that provides for our chicken and geese. This is Bella's aunt's game bird casserole recipe, which is delicious served with carrot purée and roast potatoes, or just mashed potatoes to soak up the rich gravy. We use pheasant, but it will work equally well for most wild game birds.

2 tablespoons sunflower oil

50g/3½ tablespoons butter

1 good-sized pheasant, guinea fowl or other wild game bird

100g/3½oz (7-8 slices) streaky bacon, chopped

40g/4¾ tablespoons plain/all-purpose flour

300ml/1¼ cups stock

300ml/1¼ cups red wine

2 tablespoons Bramley apple jelly

1 tablespoon Worcestershire sauce

1 teaspoon chopped fresh thyme

16 shallots, peeled, halved if large

salt and freshly ground black pepper

*SERVES 4*

Preheat the oven to 170°C/350°F/Gas 3. Heat the oil and the butter in a large heavy-based pan, add the game bird and fry quickly to brown the meat on all sides.

Lift the bird out onto a plate and leave to one side. Fry the bacon in the pan for about 3 minutes, then use a slotted spoon to transfer it to the plate with the bird. Stir the flour into the remaining fat in the pan and cook for 1 minute. Gradually add the stock and the wine and bring to the boil, stirring until thickened. Add the remaining ingredients.

Return the bird and the bacon to the pan, cover with a lid and bring back to the boil. Simmer for 5 minutes. Transfer the casserole to the preheated oven and cook for 3 hours. When tender, lift the bird out of the pan and take the meat off the bone. Return the meat to the sauce and serve, or allow the casserole to cool if you are planning to freeze it.

BELOW AND ABOVE LEFT *After picking, gooseberries are frozen on trays. We then store portions of approximately 250g/9oz of fruit (a useful cooking portion) in freezer bags, sucking out any excess air with a straw so that they are vacuum packed. This method works well for many soft fruits, including raspberries, blackberries and currants, and prevents them from sticking together and freezing into one big unwieldy lump.*

## STORING IN THE FREEZER

We have upright freezers and we have chest freezers. We have had expensive models as well as cheap ones. And we have tried our hands at freezing most of our produce. We are not experts, but nevertheless the following may be of some use to you.

Somewhere cool such as a cellar is a good place to keep a freezer, as its constant low temperature assists in the economic running of the machine. However, damp can be a problem as, exacerbated by the cold, condensation can build up on the machine and, depending on where it drains to, may lead to electrical shorting. We had one freezer that would regularly trip our whole electrical system. We got rid of it and have not had a similar problem since.

A temperature display is reassuring but not essential, as is a light to show that the machine is powered up. We run at least two freezers most of the year, but in midsummer, when we've eaten much of the previous years's meat and are yet to freeze much garden produce or harvest game, we will combine the contents in one machine and switch the other one off until it's needed again.

Chest freezers are inexpensive to run, but will accumulate a whole host of mysterious unmarked objects in their darkest corners. An annual clean-out and cook-up is a good idea. Upright freezers frequently have ill-fitting drawers and shelves that result in curses and painful toes if dropped. Neither type is perfect, but a full freezer in late autumn – the result of a summer of grazing lambs and fattened pigs, plus the harvests from the kitchen garden and fruit cages – will keep us fed all winter and well into the following year, whatever challenges the weather and the economy throw at us.

Accurately labelling produce is important, as is secure bagging. We double-bag 'bony' game like jointed rabbit to avoid punctures, and attach a label stating the contents and the date in between the two bags. Remove as much air as possible from the second bag (use a drinking straw) to prevent frost from forming, as once hidden beneath a frosty layer produce all too easily loses its identity.

For fish, freezer tubing can be purchased online – simply drop in an individual fish and knot the tube at each end before labelling. Purchasing a roll at the start of the season is an act of faith in one's fish-catching ability. 'Grip seal' pouches are perfect for storing soups and stocks, and work much better than the ubiquitous plastic box.

After a number of years of freezing, we now freeze more meat than vegetables. Two butchered pigs fill one large upright freezer, while another holds lamb, fish, poultry and game. Meat and fish freeze well, but vegetables are more temperamental – the high water content means that once frozen their structure breaks down irreparably, with a consequent loss of texture. Thus most of our harvested vegetables are eaten fresh and only frozen when batch processed or cooked. The same is true of strawberries, which spend their days in the freezer as ice cream.

We freeze soft fruit such as raspberries, gooseberries, blackberries and currants first on a tray in a single layer. Once completely frozen, they are transferred to a bag or box from which they may be shaken out individually at a later date without coagulating into a great fruity mass.

OPPOSITE ABOVE RIGHT *Foil containers/pans with lids work well for freezing batch-cooked meals as they can be neatly stacked. If you write the contents and date on the lid in pencil (not pen, as it rubs off when wet), you'll know exactly what you have frozen and where to find it.*

RIGHT *When cool, meat and vegetable stocks and homemade soups are poured into liquid freezer bags. We find these are more practical than rigid plastic containers, as they pack down neatly and take up less space.*

# Making ice cream

When we have a glut of soft fruit in the autumn, we often use it to make ice cream. It's a simple way of turning large quantities of freshly picked berries into something that freezes well, so you can enjoy the taste of summer over the months to come. Making ice cream is also a good way to use up any frozen fruit lurking at the back of the freezer.

### SUMMER FRUIT SORBET-STYLE ICE CREAM

250g/2½ cups redcurrants (picked earlier in the summer and frozen)

250g/2 cups raspberries (late autumn varieties have a lovely full flavour)

100g/¾ cup blackberries (freshly foraged from the bushes)

225g/1½ cups golden caster/superfine sugar

100ml/½ cup crème fraîche

*MAKES 1 litre/1¾ pints*

Place the fruit in a heavy-based stainless steel pan over a low heat and pour in the golden caster/superfine sugar. Add a tablespoon of water. Leave to simmer until the fruit softens. Allow to cool.

Using the back of a spoon, push the fruit through a sieve into a mixing bowl. Transfer the fruit purée to a shallow plastic container and place in the freezer for a couple of hours until it begins to freeze. Take it out, whisk in the crème fraîche and return it to the freezer for a further four hours to freeze hard.

### OLD-FASHIONED CUSTARD-STYLE ICE CREAM

300ml/1¼ cups single/ light cream

vanilla pod, sliced in half

4 egg yolks

125g/⅔ cup golden caster/ superfine sugar

300ml/1¼ cups double/ heavy cream

350g/3¼ cups soft fruit, simmered and strained to make purée (see left)

*MAKES 1 litre/1¾ pints*

Pour the single/light cream into a pan and add the vanilla pod. Place over a low heat until the cream starts to steam, but do not let it bubble. Remove from the heat.

Put the yolks and sugar in a bowl and whisk until pale and creamy. Discard the vanilla pod, then pour the warm cream into the egg mixture and whisk with a balloon whisk until smooth. Pour back into the pan and, using a wooden spoon, stir over a low heat to make a custard. To check if the custard is ready, take the spoon out of the pan and draw your finger across it – it will leave a clear line if the custard has thickened.

Strain the custard into a jug/pitcher and leave to cool to room temperature. When cool, transfer to the fridge to chill. After 30 minutes, remove and stir in the double/heavy cream.

Pour the cold fruit purée into the custard and cream mixture and combine well. Then either use an ice-cream maker to churn the mixture until it freezes, or pour it into a shallow plastic container and place in the freezer. Take it out of the freezer every hour to stir the frozen sides into the liquid centre of the ice cream. Repeat three or four times, then leave the ice-cream in the freezer to set solid.

OPPOSITE *Bella bought this cream settling pan at a local agricultural auction and has always relished the opportunity to use it for its intended purpose. When filled with unhomogenized milk, the cream settles on top within a few hours. It is then skimmed off and used to make butter while the milk is used in yoghurt-making (see page 164).*

RIGHT *Once the butter is made and has been salted to taste, Bella packs it into ramekin dishes and runs a fork over the surface to make a simple pattern. Salted butter will keep in the fridge for a week.*

# The Dairy

Part of what is now our kitchen was quite likely purpose built as a dairy, with the other end serving as a bakery in the days when the kitchen was at the front of the house. This space has the advantage of cool north walls and small windows and, before a previous owner 'modernized' the interior, what was originally a brick or quarry-tiled floor.

The room would have been minimally furnished, and easy to keep clean, and it is the only ground-floor room without its own fireplace, as it neither required heating nor would it benefit from the inevitable wood ash, dust and smuts created by an open fire. The plain walls would have had a few simple shelves to hold milk jugs/pitchers, cream settling pans and other necessary equipment.

Nowadays, the original 'cool' dairy forms part of our homestead kitchen and here we make our own salted butter, creamy natural yogurt and ice creams at the long refectory table, which is in effect an 'island' work station. We plug in labour-saving electrical devices close by and carry them to the table as and when required.

## FRESH BUTTER

The secret of really good, creamy butter that's full of flavour is the quality of the cream used to make it. Although we've often entertained the idea of having our own milk cow, it's something we've never been brave enough to do, as neither of us would relish the twice-daily milking routine.

However, we are lucky enough to have the wonderful Hook & Son Dairy very close by, a small family-run producer that sells exceptional double/heavy cream, raw (unprocessed, unpasteurized and unhomogenized) milk and raw butter from their organic grass-fed herd of pedigree Holstein Friesians. Like them, we've discovered that the secret of good butter-making is churning thoroughly and washing the butter to remove as much of the buttermilk as possible. We then use a good-quality flaky sea salt to season our butter.

Other good butters to try include those produced by the award-winning Abernethy Butter Company in Northern Ireland. Unfortunately, retail sale of raw dairy products is prohibited in some US states, but it might be worth asking about local suppliers at a local farmer's market or searching online under 'raw milk' or 'real milk'.

# Making your own butter

This is the method we used to make our first batch of butter, under the guidance of Alison Walker from *Country Living* magazine. The double/heavy cream needs to be shaken or beaten until the buttermilk and butterfat separate. This can be done in an old-fashioned churn, by shaking the cream vigorously in a screw-topped jar (which takes at least half an hour) or, by far the easiest and quickest method, using a freestanding food mixer.

**1.2 litres/5 cups double/heavy cream**
*MAKES about 600g/2¾ cups butter and 600ml/
2½ cups buttermilk*

Remove the cream from the refrigerator an hour or two before you want to make the butter and allow it to come to room temperature.

Pour the cream into the bowl of a freestanding mixer with the whisk or beater attachment in place. Start to beat on medium speed. Keep watching as the cream will suddenly separate into big clumps of butter and a pool of buttermilk – the time this takes will depend on the temperature of the room and the age of the cream you are using.

Strain off the buttermilk through a muslin-lined sieve into a bowl and chill until needed. You can drink it or use it to make buttermilk scones, pancakes or soda bread.

Put the lumps of butter in a colander, place under cold running water and gently squeeze and knead the butter to remove excess buttermilk. The liquid squeezed out will gradually run clear. This stage is essential as any buttermilk left in the butter will sour and go rancid quickly. Using butter pats or paddles will squeeze out the liquid in the same way and form it into blocks.

To make salted butter, add a scant ¼ teaspoon of flaky salt and knead it in thoroughly. Taste the butter – if it's too salty, rinse it under cold water again. Shape it into a log and wrap in greaseproof paper. Unsalted butter keeps for 2–3 days in the fridge; salted butter for up to a week; both can be frozen for up to one month.

# Making yogurt

In Bella's house back in the 1970s, there always seemed to be a flask of yogurt sitting in the airing cupboard/linen closet alongside the school shirts. Bella's mother, in her Biba kaftan and matching headscarf, enjoyed making it but it always seemed a dark art – the ability to convert the last scrapings of the yogurt pot into a new pot of the stuff.

Nowadays, live yogurt is considered essential to good health, thanks to its gut-enhancing bacteria. You can buy yogurt starter cultures in dried form online or in health food shops, but a small pot of live, plain, preferably organic yogurt will do the same job. And it will contain enough bacteria to transform a litre/quart or more of milk. To achieve a thick, creamy yogurt, use milk that has a high fat content, such as full-fat cow's milk, and add powdered milk to make it even thicker.

**1 litre/4½ cups full-fat milk**

**50g/²⁄₃ cup powdered milk**

**150ml/5fl oz live plain yogurt, preferably organic, at room temperature**

*MAKES 500ml/16fl oz*

Pour the milk into a saucepan and whisk in the powdered milk. If your milk is pasteurized, heat it to 85°C/ 185°F, stirring occasionally, then leave the milk to cool to about 46°C/115°F (this results in thicker yogurt and takes about 30 minutes). You'll need a thermometer for this. Then gradually whisk or stir in the live yogurt.

Before the mixture cools, pour it into a warmed wide-mouth vacuum flask and screw on the lid. Leave it for seven hours or even longer if you want thick, stronger tasting yogurt. After the allotted time, spoon the yogurt out of the vacuum flask into clean jars and store them in the refrigerator. The yogurt will keep for up to five days.

# The Pantry

A pantry can be as simple as a dedicated cupboard, or as grand as an entire room of its own. It is one of those rooms of utility, including mud rooms, boot rooms and laundry rooms, that are so often overlooked yet form the core of the successful domestic household.

Nick grew up in a house that had a kitchen with a basic larder cupboard that was just a white-painted wooden box attached to the outside of a north-facing kitchen wall. A perforated zinc panel provided ventilation and a large wooden door afforded access from inside the kitchen. It was a sturdy structure (in fact strong enough to support a small boy climbing to the roof above), but an equally keen and nimble burglar could perhaps have removed the zinc and gained easy access to the kitchen, pausing only to help himself to a slice of pie on the way.

Ideally a pantry will be sited in the coolest part of the house with ventilation to the exterior, yet close to the kitchen. A large cupboard could be converted into a pantry, or part of a utility or boot room adapted. Cool stone shelves and tiled walls help to reduce the internal temperature and are easy to keep clean. Lots of narrow shelves ensure the contents are visible from the entrance and nothing is permitted to hide at the back. A light is useful to admire the contents and to reveal the presence of any late-night raiders feasting within.

LEFT *The pantry is a place of great interest and importance in our house. Even a large cupboard lined with food on shelves has an allure for small children (or children 'of all ages'), and ours are often to be found raiding their grandmother's walk-in pantry. If feeling particularly in need of comfort, they will shut the door behind them and munch silently and unseen.*

## PRESERVING VEGETABLES

One of Nick's earliest memories is of stringing and slicing runner beans to be salted down for the coming winter. Alternate layers of salt and beans were added to glass jars and sealed. The salt drew out the moisture content of the beans, which were then removed by the handful and rinsed of salt before boiling as and when needed. He doesn't remember them tasting great, but that may have been because he had them at every other meal!

On the homestead, we grow borlotti/cranberry and Soissons beans up a frame of coppiced hazel poles. Those we don't eat fresh are left on the vine to dry. Once the withered pods are brittle, we cut them down and lay them on racks to dry. We shell the beans onto trays and leave them to dry further. Finally, we jar them up and store them in the pantry. To rehydrate the beans, soak them in water overnight, then simmer them in boiling water for 20 minutes before adding to stews and soups.

We still have Nick's father's wooden measure for gauging the smallest shallots for pickling, but we prefer to eat them cooked. We do make our own pickle, or rather chutney. The words are often used interchangeably, but a pickle is generally a raw vegetable preserved in brine, vinegar or oil, while a chutney involves cooking. It is a favourite way to use up all those excess golden courgettes/zucchini, and green tomatoes with apples and onions. All the excess of autumn is in a jar.

## Making chutney

This is a courgette/zucchini chutney mix with plenty of dried fruit. The recipe was originally one of Sarah Raven's, but we have tweaked and adapted it over the years.

1.8kg/4lb yellow courgettes/zucchini, diced into 5cm/2in cubes

2 x green apples, diced into 5cm/2in cubes

500ml/2 cups white wine vinegar

500g/3¾ cups mixed chopped dried apricots, raisins and cranberries

500g/2½ cups soft brown sugar

½ teaspoon black peppercorns

1 teaspoon each of mustard seeds, allspice, ground ginger and chilli flakes/hot pepper flakes

*MAKES 12–15 jars*

Place the courgettes/zucchini and apples in a large preserving pan. Add the vinegar, dried fruits and sugar, and stir. Place all the spices in a muslin bag. Submerge the bag in the pan and leave overnight.

The following day, simmer the chutney over a low heat for at least one hour (but several hours is best) until it is rich and dark. Stir occasionally so that it doesn't burn on the bottom. Discard the spice bag. Spoon the chutney into sterilized jars (we use Kilner or Mason preserving jars).

# Making fruit leather

Excess orchard fruit can be stored, cut into rings and dried, or made into jellies and chutneys, but another way of preserving it is to make fruit leather. Bella's mother always has a surplus of plums from her orchard and these form the basis of a good fruit leather, blended with any other available fruit.

6 plums

3 small eating apples

3 pears

*MAKES one tray of fruit leather (about 15 rolls)*

Stone the plums. Core the apples and pears but do not peel them. Put the fruit into a food processor and blend it to a smooth pulp. Alternatively, we use our hand-operated mincer to mash the fruit finely.

Once the fruit is reduced to a smooth pulp, drain off any excess liquid (we use this to make ice lollies/popsicles) and spread the mixture on lined baking sheets in a thin layer about 1cm/½in thick. Use a knife or spatula to even it out, so it all dries at the same rate. The thinner the layer, the quicker the leather will dry. We place ours in the bottom oven of the range oven or in an electric oven at the very lowest setting, as the mixture needs to dry out but not cook. We leave it in the oven overnight or for about eight to ten hours.

Once it has reduced to a rubbery consistency, lift with a spatula and roll into a tube, then slice the tube into pieces 5cm/2in wide. Store in a sealed clip-top jar. It should keep long enough to enjoy over the winter, unrolling and tearing off pieces as desired.

# The Cellar

From the 'new' kitchen, worn brick steps lead down to a brick and sandstone-lined cellar dug out beneath what was originally the front parlour and is now the library. The door originally had a lock, as when the house was built this was an exterior door, and we still keep it locked, if only to prevent the unwary from falling down the stairs and 'unauthorized access' to the preserved produce contained within. Here, whatever the weather and throughout the year, the temperature remains constant, never rising too high even during the hottest of summers, as the cellar is insulated by the surrounding cool Wealden clay.

Ours is a 'damp' cellar – we have not tried to tame it with waterproof tanked walls and floors, but a pump sits in a sump hole in the corner and automatically pumps ground water out into the field should it threaten to rise. Along the interior walls are cut brick and stone-lined niches, which form storage shelves, and on top of the brick floor we have added practical duckboarding, which allows a bare or socked foot comfortable access even during the wettest of winters. Additional shelving lines the cool interior wall, while our well-stocked freezers occupy the wall closest to the staircase.

This is not necessarily a place to linger, in part because the ceiling is low, and one always runs the risk that some mischievous family member will turn the lock and leave one incarcerated. However, each Christmas we use the cellar as a bar at our Twelfth Night party, and it is briefly the most sought-after room in the house.

RIGHT *Our cool, damp cellar runs from north to south along the east side of the house. It is rather beautiful in its monastic simplicity and is the ideal space for storing glassware and red wine, for which it is the perfect temperature. Our only addition to this space was the treated duckboarding we laid on top of the damp, bare-brick floor.*

# Making switchel

Switchel is a refreshing, old-fashioned cordial that's easy to prepare and can be kept cool in the cellar or refrigerator until needed. On warm days, we dilute it with fizzy water to make a 'spritzel', although purists might prefer it with still. It goes particularly well with vodka too, or rum, if you're feeling piratical.

1 heaped tablespoon grated
  fresh root ginger

1 tablespoon honey

2 tablespoons apple cider vinegar

*MAKES 1 litre/3¹/4 cups when diluted
  with sparkling water*

We are unable to grow root ginger here as we don't have a heated glasshouse, but we use our own honey and local apple cider vinegar.

Place a generous tablespoon of freshly grated ginger in a sterilized clip-top jar with a rubber seal. Add the honey and apple cider vinegar. Seal and leave the cordial to steep overnight in a cool place (we place it in the cellar).

Who knows whether former inhabitants of our little homestead used to drink a similar elixir from the cellar on hot summer mornings after an early start cutting grass for hay? Boiled and bruised ginger was used to flavour mead (a drink made from honey and yeast) in the early 1700s, and this is a pleasant but complex-flavoured, non-alcoholic alternative for the hard-working labourer.

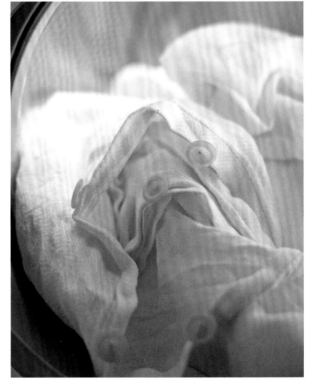

# Homestead Housekeeping

It cannot be denied that old houses are harder to maintain, and this one is no exception. The beamed ceilings attract cobwebs and dust, while the open fires, wood-fuelled rayburn, dogs and children all increase the dirt exponentially. Where possible, we like to use mainly natural products to clean the house, including our own beeswax furniture polish and linseed oil floor wash, together with plenty of fresh air to dry the laundry and ventilate the rooms.

## LAUNDRY

One of our pet hates is heavily perfumed washing detergent and fabric conditioners that smell artificially 'clean'. Baking soda, vinegar, borax, lemon juice and hydrogen peroxide will all keep your clothes bone white. Add half a cup of any of these cleaners to the washing drum of your machine before running a wash cycle. For double duty, add half a cup of borax to the washing drum of the machine and half a cup of vinegar to your rinse drawer before washing a white load. Both ingredients will brighten whites, and the vinegar will soften your clothes.

To restore dingy or grey whites, soak articles in 4½ litres /1 gallon of hot water mixed with half a cup of washing soda/soda crystals, then launder as usual. Finally, try to hang your clothes out to dry in the sun – an inexpensive natural whitener. It will naturally bleach garments without setting stains like a dryer.

When drying outside isn't possible, we use our 'Airy Fairy' dryer – it's a wooden contraption a bit like a pulley maid that's designed to use the warmth of the kitchen to dry clothes. However, rather than hanging from the beamed ceiling, which is fairly low, the Airy Fairy hooks onto the front rail of our Rayburn range cooker and uses the heat radiating from the metal doors to dry the laundry hanging on its wooden bars – ingenious.

**OPPOSITE ABOVE LEFT**
*A folding canvas bucket has become a useful, if unusual, peg bag. It can fold up concertina-style to almost nothing or even dangle casually over your forearm, hands-free, when pegging out laundry.*

**OPPOSITE ABOVE RIGHT**
*We have two 8m-/26ft-long washing lines that extend from a detachable grey drum on the north wall of the house and stretch across the garden to our Asian pear tree. This is where we dry large sheets and duvet covers on bright and breezy wash days.*

**OPPOSITE BELOW LEFT**
*Freshly laundered and well-ironed bed linen is one of life's great luxuries. Even if we have little time to iron clothes, we always find time to iron bed linen so our bed is always welcoming at the end of a long day.*

**OPPOSITE BELOW RIGHT**
*Old white linen duvet covers and sheets take on a wonderful soft texture as they age.*

**LEFT** *When the weather is too wet to hang washing out to dry, we drape damp items on the wooden 'Airy Fairy' clotheshorse in front of the Rayburn range cooker. The heat of the range dries laundry quickly, so this is a good energy-saving solution.*

# Making natural beeswax furniture polish

A wonderful by-product of keeping bees, leftover shavings of pure beeswax can be used to make natural furniture polish and beauty balm.

  The polish we like is very simple and requires just two main ingredients – beeswax and olive oil – unlike some recipes that include turpentine. Olive oil on its own is very effective as a wood polish, but in combination with beeswax it becomes more durable and produces a longer-lasting result. The inclusion of clear grapefruit seed extract adds antioxidants that prevent the olive oil from turning rancid and keep this delicious polish from losing its rich, honey-scented beeswax aroma.

150g/$^2$/$_3$ cup beeswax
600g/3 cups olive oil
30 drops grapefruit-seed extract
  (a natural antioxidant)
10 drops lavender essential oil
*MAKES three 100ml/3$^1$/$_2$fl oz tins*

Put the beeswax and olive oil into a double boiler or bain-marie. (A double boiler can be made by floating a small heatproof glass bowl inside a saucepan filled with hot water.) It is important to heat the beeswax and oil in this way because it is safer (wax is flammable) and it helps to retain the natural qualities of the ingredients.

  Heat the double boiler over a medium heat until the oil and beeswax are completely melted. Don't burn the mixture and ruin it. Add the grapefruit seed extract and the lavender essential oil and stir well.

  Pour the hot mixture into clean containers. Allow to cool for at least two hours, until the mixture forms a semi-hard balm consistency.

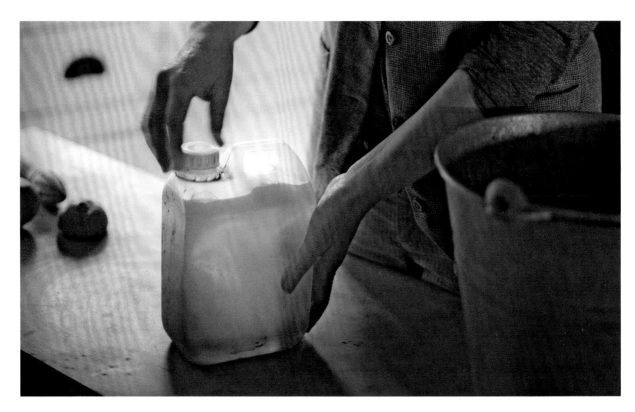

# Linseed oil floor cleaner

The bare oak floorboards in our farmhouse are subject to heavy traffic. Our favourite floor cleaner is a home-made solution based on linseed oil soap, which can be bought at art supply stores, builder's merchants or online. Linseed oil soap has a rich, almost nutty fragrance and, like beeswax polish or even wood smoke, it never fails to instill a sense of calm.

We use this home-made floor cleaner every few days to mop the wooden boards throughout the farmhouse. We add a few drops of essential oil (such as lavender) to the floor cleaner, as well as white wine vinegar or lemon juice, which help to remove stains and lift dirt very effectively.

2 tablespoons/⅛ cup linseed oil soap (or a vegetable-oil detergent if you live in a hard-water area)

120ml/½ cup white wine vinegar or lemon juice

3-4 drops of lavender essential oil, as desired

9 litres/2 gallons warm water

Combine all the ingredients in a pail or bucket. Swirl the warm water around until suds appear. If you live in a hard-water area, the minerals in the water will cause a slippery scum to form when combined with linseed oil, so you will need to add a commercial detergent-based soap instead.

If you don't want to make your own floor cleaner, there are a couple of natural floor soaps made with linseed oil on the market. If you are buying a commercial linseed oil floor cleaner, the key is to choose one that is made without artificial solvents or fragrances.

# The Utility Room

*A utility room with a large sink is invaluable for all sorts of messy tasks, such as rewaxing our cotton work jackets and thawing out the animal water drinkers well away from the kitchen.*

Skinning, plucking and drawing are undertaken outside on the porch, but fish gutting always takes place inside in the utility sink. It could be done in the kitchen, but as we are generally still dressed in our fishy finery it seems better to work here, then we can undress straight into the laundry basket and sprint upstairs for a bath and fresh clothes.

As well as providing a home to the sink and the laundry, the utility room is home to our sewing kit. This is a manly affair, full of triangular, pointed, razor-edged leather needles, curved upholstery and sailmaker's needles, and button thread so strong that it will cut into the fingers if trying to 'pull for a break'. Swatches of canvas and oilskin lie in wait to patch a hole. A dainty tin contains salvaged buttons and screw-in studs, for extra grip in boots and waders.

The utility room would be a good home for glues and household tools, but ours are generally kept in the workshop. The same goes for a basic first-aid kit, which in our case is divided between the fridge (medicines) and bathroom cabinet (plasters).

OPPOSITE *Nick is something of a master tailor and repairer – his stitching is neat and his patience enduring. His tasks include sewing on buttons and patching waxed jackets or canvas bags as part of our 'make do and mend' approach.*

ABOVE LEFT *Rubber waders are given extra gripping power with screw-in studs, available from angling suppliers. Nick uses his multi tool Leatherman to secure them in place at the start of the fishing season.*

ABOVE CENTRE *The leather soles of these walking boots have come unstitched around the toe. To increase their working life, Nick uses a strong waterproof adhesive and a clamp to fasten the sole in place until the glue has firmly bonded.*

ABOVE RIGHT *Wax is used to re-waterproof cotton jackets. To make it easier to apply, melt the wax first by placing the unopened tin in a pan or bowl of hot water. Lots of thin coats applied with a brush work better than one thick coat of wax.*

# The Boot Room

*The boot room is one of those transitional zones, like the porch, that are so essential on a hard-working homestead. It is a place for storing all types of clothing required for all kinds of weather, as well as our huge collection of boots. It is a place for drying footwear plus outer clothing and hats, riding and fishing kit, and, of course, dogs.*

You could argue that all these tasks could be undertaken elsewhere, such as outside on the porch or even inside beside the kitchen fire. But no – for the chief purpose of the boot room is the containment of mud.

The boot room comes into its own during the wet, dark winter months. During summer we enjoy spending time on the porch, but in winter the boot room is our saviour. Autumn rains turn the dusty patch beneath the hazel copse into a quagmire, and wet mud sucks at the feet, threatening to pull off one's boots with every step. The boot room is a place to disrobe and deboot. Wet and muddy gear is removed at the door and hung up, ready for when needed again.

It is easy for a clutter of discarded clogs, boots and shoes to build up at the door and trip the unwary, so some sort of shelving system is required here. We stack tall muddy boots in a neat row against the wall at ground level. Above them, shelves hold any footwear that is clean enough to pick up without soiling the hands. A beam at ceiling level outside on the porch provides a home for any boots that are kept in reserve, but those regularly required are rewarded by a place in the boot room.

ABOVE LEFT *The sturdy metal hooks on the back of the door are used to hang up wet things, including Nick's waders after a day's fishing. Our boot room doors have rows of hooks on wood batons, some of which were already in situ when we arrived at Walnuts Farm, and some of which we've added.*

ABOVE *Waxed and padded jackets for young and old alike hang on the back of the door. An extra layer is usually required, even when we are just popping outside to collect something from one of the outbuildings.*

OPPOSITE *There is something very pleasing about a row of well-polished boots. Most of our outdoor leather footwear is on display on open shelves so that it can be quickly pulled out or put away.*

LEFT *This area is designed to be both useful and pleasing to the eye, with everything well ordered and in its place. Our collection of leather dog leads and collars, a rope lamb halter, and a leather fly swat hang from a row of small hooks. Other items for outdoor pursuits include felt hats, netted bags for foraging and fishing, binoculars in a sturdy leather case, drawers stuffed full of gloves and a walking stick.*

ABOVE *Our hinged wooden box full of polish and brushes is a treasured item made by Nick's father when he was a boy especially for this purpose. The smell of the polish is nostalgic, and cleaning and buffing a pair of boots with a bristle brush is a job that both children and adults seem to find rewarding.*

Hooks on the backs of the doors hold coats, waistcoats/vests, leggings and over-trousers, together with hats of all kinds. We could add more hooks to the walls to house our entire collection, but instead we operate a seasonal system, storing our winter coats upstairs in the wardrobe during summer, and swapping them for lightweight waterproofs as the seasons change. Gloves are stowed in pairs in a drawer beside the door, along with torches for late-night animal feeds or salad hunts. Beneath the drawers, the wet dogs lie on waterproof beds, which can be moved beside the fire when desired. Dog-training gear, spare collars, leads and sundries are all housed in a collection of net-fronted bags and canvas buckets that hang beneath the coats.

We hang up wet coats and other items in the porch and then, when they have stopped dripping, bring them into the kitchen to slowly dry off, hanging from one of the many hooks in the ceiling beams or around the fireplace. We have misplaced our home-made bootjack and currently have to rely on the doorstep, threshold or the edge of the porch deck instead. Meanwhile, various ornamental boot-scrapers decorate the entrances, but are frequently neglected in use.

Boot polishes of all colours and vintages, saddle soaps and an old button-polishing guard (which last saw action in 1945) are housed in a white-painted wooden box. Beside the door is an empty space on a marble-topped dresser, but it is rarely empty long, for here lives that collection of items deemed to be 'in transit' and destined for delivery to the workshop, shed or garden.

# The Sitting Room

*After a day working outside in the open, a cosy, dark sitting room with the aromatic embers of a wood fire burning in the grate is a very seductive place to be. Our inspiration for the sitting room was the smoking room at a traditional English gentlemen's club or a 17th-century Dutch merchant's house. It is a masculine, pared-back style, which appeals to us both. In the early evening, the fading light slants across the wooden floor, the fire crackles as it burns, the beeswax candle and electric table lamps glow, and the inglenook fireplace is so deep that you can comfortably tuck your armchair in close to the wood-burner.*

ABOVE, ABOVE RIGHT AND OPPOSITE *As this room is small and the ceiling is low, we have only a few pieces of simple furniture in here. We prefer the room to be underlit (by table lamps and the light of the fire), rather* than overlit. The walls are painted in Farrow & Ball's 'Down Pipe' for a cosy, clubbable feel. Soft furnishings are limited to an old kilim rug and ottoman and a Roman blind/shade made from Ian Mankin charcoal-grey linen ticking.

ABOVE *The bucket chair is upholstered in a sage-green velvet and is very good at supporting the back. It is a favourite chair for both of us as well as for Blink, the grey whippet, at the end of a long day.*

The colour scheme in here is dark grey and bitter chocolate. The narrow Georgian sofa was reupholstered in a dark-chocolate Hungarian linen bought inexpensively at a haberdashery shop in the nearby town of St Leonards-on-Sea. The floor is simple painted hardboard and the matt black floor paint has become so scratched and scuffed that it looks rather like old slate or stone, but has the advantage that it is warm to walk on.

We have no overhead lighting here, just two table lamps and a standard lamp. And we have to confess that we do have a postage-stamp-sized television but it is kept hidden away in a large built-in cupboard.

LEFT *The wall above the sofa is hung with a collection of Dutch-style rural scenes and Hogarth prints that add to the intimate atmosphere of our dark sitting room. We like paintings and prints arranged in groups and rarely hang a painting on its own. Ideally, every inch of wall would be covered from top to bottom. Some of the paintings and prints were inherited, while others were bought at local auctions or antiques markets.*

ABOVE *A collection of daguerreotypes portraying Nick's relatives from the 1840s onwards are arranged along the top of a grey box, formerly an agricultural toolbox found at an auction. The box now houses our collection of family photos before they are stuck into albums – a good project for those long, dark winter evenings.*

# The perfect fire

Laying a good fire that can be lit with just a match rather than a firelighter is an art in itself. You'll need plenty of bone-dry tinder, such as dry bracken or moss, crumpled newspaper, wood shavings and dry twigs, to start with.

Put a large handful of tinder right in the centre of the grate, preferably on a bed of ash. On top of this, build a square base of dry kindling. Start with two parallel sticks about the thickness of a thumb. On top of these, place another pair of parallel sticks to form a square. Continue to stack the kindling in layers. Now place two or three well-seasoned small logs on top of the kindling. Light the tinder with a match and watch the flames take hold. As this structure catches and starts to burn down, you can add larger logs.

**TRADITIONAL FIREWOOD POEM**

Beechwood fires burn bright and clear
If the logs are kept a year;
Store your beech for Christmastide
With new-cut holly laid beside;
Chestnut's only good, they say,
If for years 'tis stored away;
Birch and fir-wood burn too fast
Blaze too bright and do not last;
Flames from larch will shoot up high,
Dangerously the sparks will fly;
But ash-wood green and ash-wood brown
Are fit for a Queen with a golden crown.

Oaken logs, if dry and old,
Keep away the winter's cold;
Poplar gives a bitter smoke,
Fills your eyes and makes you choke;
Elm-wood burns like churchyard mould,
E'en the very flames are cold;
It is by the Irish said;
Hawthorn bakes the sweetest bread,
Apple-wood will scent the room,
Pear-wood smells like flowers in bloom;
But ash-wood wet and ash-wood dry
A King may warm his slippers by.

*Celia Congreve*
*First published in* The Times, *March 1930*

**ABOVE** *Bella believes this large cut-out of a Suffolk Punch horse once stood above a brewery when these dray/draft horses delivered barrels of beer on carts. Or perhaps it might have been a pub sign. Who knows exactly, but it has followed her everywhere, from a small London apartment to a tiny cottage and now to Walnuts Farm. She has always managed to find a bare wall large enough to hold it.*

**LEFT** *Nick made this simple ship from a piece of hardwood that reminded him of the hull of a boat. He added a lick of grey paint and two red cylinders that once were part of his childhood building-block set. Our daughter Flora stuck on paper circles to make portholes and their wonky placement adds to the naïvety and charm of the piece.*

**OPPOSITE BELOW** *This yeoman farmer, Friesian cow and young colt were found at a vintage fair. They were probably children's toys originally, part of a larger set of farm pieces. We were drawn to their simple cut-out shapes and painted surfaces, and they make for a pleasing arrangement on a windowsill in our simple farmhouse interior.*

## FOLK ART IN THE FARMHOUSE

We like to surround ourselves with art, often animal and landscape in subject and origin. Images of animals and the land, and found objects from it – both in the immediate vicinity and wider landscape – are all around us. I sometimes wonder if this is our equivalent of 'cave art', and whether we are creating and collecting for a similar purpose.

In our dark sitting room hang Dutch and East Anglian school landscapes showing watermills, farmsteads and hard-working country homes. They are a source of both inspiration during the long winter months and reflection on past lives and a common ancestral inheritance. Some pieces were inherited and others were found at local auctions and car-boot fairs/yard sales, but increasingly we are creating our own art too. Over the long winter nights we might add to our collection, fashioning cut-out animals from plywood and sheet metal. In early spring we cast trophy fish in plaster, and in autumn we seek abandoned birds' nests while trimming the hedges.

The traditional Britains model farm and animals were an early influence upon Nick, and his father even cast his own herd of dairy cattle from lead as a child in the 1930s. So perhaps it is not surprising that a selection of cut-out animals and farm models have been promoted to stand alongside the collection of finds on the mantelpiece.

In the kitchen, a print shows a prize ox, an oblong slab of ostentatious agricultural pride, residing in a pastoral idyll. It is an idealized scene, as unobtainable now as it was when it was made, but it inspires us still.

ABOVE *A painted wooden goat's head with real goat's horns sits on either side of the mirror in the library. They are a perfect example of simple folk art, and their dark-circled eyes and black noses make them resemble primitive masks.*

# Decorating with Natural Finds

We like to show our love and respect for nature by collecting objects that catch our eye and arouse our curiosity. Here at Walnuts Farm, our natural finds are a mix of birds' feathers, eggshells, flowers, decorative branches, pieces of driftwood, birds' nests and rabbit skulls unearthed in hedgerows and ditches. Like our Victorian forebears, we like to create cabinets of curiosities, frame these objects as wall art or arrange them on mantelpieces, windowsills or tabletops. Natural discoveries are to be found in every room of the farmhouse and are an integral part of what makes our home truly ours.

Our flock of poultry includes the pretty little Coturnix quail, which is both a good egg layer and a delicious meat bird. We keep the quail in a small wooden ark on the kitchen-garden beds, where they scratch about and do some helpful weeding and manuring. This location – close to the house – also provides shelter from the elements and predators, as these little birds are less hardy than larger poultry and more prone to predator attack.

Quail lay their eggs in shallow depressions on bare soil, so they can sometimes be difficult to spot as they are so well camouflaged. The eggs have a lovely creamy texture and are best cooked for just a couple of minutes in boiling water, then served cold with celery salt. Children love them, as they are a more manageable size than chicken eggs and easy for small hands to peel. The eggs are also extremely pretty, with their mottled markings and lovely brown splodges and spots, so we often blow extra eggs for use in decorative projects.

LEFT *Quail are good layers and from Valentine's Day onwards, as the daylight hours increase, you'll be rewarded with an egg a day from each hen. We usually keep about six birds, as all the family enjoy the eggs.*

# Decorative quail egg art

We like to bring the outdoors in to mark the changing seasons, and the natural beauty of quail eggs makes them an obvious choice for our natural style of interior decoration. Here, eggs have been blown, then displayed in a deep frame to create a 'museum specimen' effect.

**9 quail eggs**

**pin**

**drinking straw**

**strong glue**

**small paintbrush**

**square box frame**
from Ikea or similar, approximately 25 x 25cm/ 10 x 10in

To blow the quail eggs, use a pin to make a small hole at the top and bottom of each shell. Using a drinking straw, gently blow the albumen and yolk out through the bottom hole into a bowl. Rinse the egg through with cold running water and leave the empty shells to dry.

Mark a small 'x' in the very centre of the backing card, lay it flat and then arrange the eggs by eye. A small dab of glue is all that is needed to secure them firmly in place. While the glue is drying, we paint the frames dark grey or bitter-chocolate brown, then place the finished item in our 'cabinet of curiosities' at the top of the stairs.

# Making a snowdrop bowl

In springtime, the first flowers to appear on the homestead are a mass of snowdrops (*Galanthus nivalis*) among the woodstack – a sure sign that spring is on its way. Snowdrops do well here and, with careful division of the bulbs and replanting over the last few years, we have managed to populate large swathes of the woodland area alongside the track that runs past the farmhouse. However, snowdrops won't always grow where you want them, and many of them have migrated to fill the damp ditches along our boundary, probably spread by seed. Lifting and planting some of the snowdrop bulbs in a shallow bowl or other container offers the perfect opportunity to bring some outdoor beauty indoors. Once the flowers have faded, we replant the bulbs outside to populate even more of our 'wild' areas with the flowers. This sort of arrangement works equally well with any small bulbs, such as *Narcissus* 'Tête-à-Tête', from the garden or even from the garden centre.

To plant up snowdrops (or any other bulbs), fill a large, shallow pan (we used a large creamware pan) with potting compost. Divide up the clumps of bulbs and push them into the compost, packing them in closely together. In nature, snowdrops seem to enjoy this close companionship and are rarely seen growing alone. Fill any gaps between the plants with damp moss – we peeled ours from the clay roof tiles on the bread oven, which is most satisfying as the moss comes away in slabs. Pack the moss around the flowers to help retain moisture, as snowdrops like rich, damp conditions, then spray the whole bowl with water before carrying it indoors. A truly gratifying, simple pleasure.

# The Library

*What we rather grandly call the library is really the old parlour, and the atmosphere of this room is still somewhat present. It is the sort of place in which we imagine previous occupants might once have entertained the local vicar to tea.*

**ABOVE AND RIGHT** *Call us old-fashioned, but we both still enjoy looking things up in books and researching and planning projects for the year ahead in the quiet, calm space of the room we call the library.*

For us, the library is a room of retreat from the hubbub of family life; somewhere to pause and admire the view southwards over the meadow in early spring, or of the lambs fattening on the grass in autumn. And it is a place to read together in the evening, with the wood-burner lit and sloe gin served in slender Georgian glasses.

The room is painted a cool, calming shade of greenish white. Bookshelves line the walls on either side of the fireplace, and housed on them are volumes on poultry and pig-keeping, lurchers and longdogs, the history of traps and trapping, as well as rows of art and angling books, and decorated cloth-bound classics for children and adults alike.

Above the Jøtul 602N wood-burner is a simple shelf upon which stands a model of a German farm girl feeding her lone gander, which has descended

OPPOSITE, ABOVE LEFT TO RIGHT *Our mantelpiece is decorated with an eclectic mix of natural objects that have personal meaning for us. The little goose girl and her goose originally belonged to Nick's grandmother, while the cottage in the photograph is where Nick's mother grew up in the 1930s. The bird's nest is beautifully made, lined with smooth mud and with an outer coat of moss. It was found abandoned in a hedge in the kitchen garden. We added the hand-blown quail's eggs for fun, but in reality quail do not nest but lay their eggs in a shallow muddy dip on the ground. The stuffed green woodpecker in a glass cabinet was found in a local junk shop.*

OPPOSITE BELOW *At Easter, we pick hazel branches and arrange them in a large container filled with water to encourage their bright green leaves to unfurl. We hang hand-blown and painted hens' eggs on ribbons from the hazel branches.*

RIGHT *The library is lighter and brighter than our sitting room and has a large gilded mirror on one wall that helps to bounce the light about.*

from a grandmother and been played with rather boisterously by each subsequent generation. Beside her is a bird's nest that contains blown quail eggs, mementoes from our honeymoon, collections of old butterflies, a stuffed green woodpecker, and family photographs from generations now lost.

A mounted buck and horned wooden goat's heads – life-size taxidermist's 'forms' once used for mounting animal heads – stare down at us from the walls, and cased beetles crawl up them. Surrounded by such items, we're reminded of our own small but significant role in this family of animals.

THIS PAGE *Pale grey and yellow are soothing colours when used in combination. Our bedroom is sparsely decorated with just a favourite oil painting, given to Bella by her grandfather, propped up on the mantelpiece and our initials in tin. Light floods in from the three south-facing windows and in winter pure wool rugs in dark colours are pulled out of the coffer to make things a little more cosy.*

# The Bedrooms

*Our bedroom interior at Walnuts Farm
is almost monastic in its simplicity. Bella
likes a room to feel uncluttered, free of all
distraction and therefore conducive to sleep.
When we first moved here we found the peace
and quiet unnerving – no aircraft, no road
traffic, no light pollution – but now we've
come to expect it and embrace it.*

All the bedrooms are pretty much the same size,
about 3.6 x 3.6m/12 x 12ft. The two south-facing
rooms are the lightest and brightest and perhaps
the most appealing in their aspect, as they look
out across the wildflower meadow to the mixed
native woodland hedgerow that marks the
boundary with the neighbouring land.

When we arrived, one of the first things Bella
did was to rip up the pale green linoleum flooring
that ran throughout the upper floor (obviously
the practical flooring solution for modern farmers
in Britain in the 1950s and 1960s) to discover

ABOVE *This south-facing bedroom is always light and bright. It is the only room where we have painted all the timber ceiling beams pure white, which turned out to be something of a labour of love as it took numerous layers of paint and plenty of man-hours!*

wonderful wide oak floor planks. We polished these with linseed oil soap solution and vinegar and have a faded old Persian rug to step out of bed onto. We have tried to keep all soft furnishings, including curtains and carpets, to a minimum, as Nick is asthmatic and this way we can keep the dust mites under control.

This room has its original fireplace (which we've never used) and two matching French grey wardrobes on either side – 'his' and 'hers'. A pretty pair of matching balloon-back chairs flanking the fireplace completes the symmetry. The chairs have woven wicker seats that are really too delicate to sit on and instead are used at the end of the day to hold discarded clothes.

Our room is lit by a single table lamp and the curtains are heavy, interlined cream silk, which retains the warmth. A large carved wooden trunk filled with wool blankets and eiderdowns sits under the window and doubles up as a window seat.

The walls are decorated with two large Georgian mirrors, one oval-shaped with an egg-and-dart moulding and the other a more ornate Swedish Gustavian example. Bella bought the latter in Liverpool and then wondered how on earth she was going to get it home! Some of the paintwork is original, including the creamy yellow window frames and fireplace surround. We have never repainted these because we wanted to keep some of the room's original paint colours.

THIS PAGE AND OPPOSITE BELOW
*We painted the floorboards black in an
attempt to even up the colour tone of the
worn, mismatched boards. A simple fold-up
chair sits in the doorway of the cupboard
that leads to the attic, and the only decoration
is Bella's Suffolk Punch horse. In the brick
fireplace recess is a leather suitcase brimming
with* cartes de visites *and old family portraits.*

ABOVE, CLOCKWISE FROM TOP LEFT *Simple curtains with tab tops hang from wooden poles in the white bedroom. The fabric was bought in a French market. We painted the brick chimney white to tie in with the rest of the room. The construction of the lateral beams interlocking with the thicker supporting beam would not have been on show when the house was built, but hidden behind a lath-and-plaster ceiling.*

The white bedroom also sits on the south side of the house and is the mirror image of our bedroom across the landing. It has a very different feel, though, as we decided to paint all the woodwork white, including the ceiling timbers, fireplace and cupboard doors. Again, the furnishings are minimal: the handmade tab top curtains are threaded onto a painted wooden pole, the floorboards are painted black and a couple of antique oval-shaped mirrors and a large Suffolk Punch horse – an old pub sign – hang on the walls. The white bedspread is Indian in origin and adds textural interest. The slingback chair covered in ticking fabric is campaign furniture – designed specifically to fold up for ease of transport for army officers.

# The Children's Bedrooms

The same simplicity of furnishings extends to the children's bedrooms, which are as minimally furnished as they will allow. By nature, most children aren't inclined to this way of being and prefer to collect, hoard and scatter, so in Flora's room we have laid large rush-matting rugs over the floorboards so they can play there. They both have large antique cupboards bought at the local auction rooms and these hold toys and games, with a chest of drawers for clothes plus wooden storage boxes under the bed for all their bits and bobs. Once again, both rooms have thick, interlined curtains to exclude draughts and block the light in high summer, when it's hard for the girls to believe it's time to go to bed.

The concept of the natural home is something that we are keen to endorse, and throughout the bedrooms we have consciously avoided man-made materials. The fibres we surround ourselves with are cotton, linen and wool, and the pillows and duvets/comforters are filled with duck down. The bedrooms are well-ventilated and we open the windows wide every morning, whatever the season. Bella regularly hangs the duvets out of the windows to give them a good airing. In bed, we follow the rule that the head should be cool and the feet warm, so an electric blanket is our guilty pleasure.

**BELOW LEFT AND RIGHT**
*Peggy's sleigh-style bed dates from the 1850s and is probably Eastern European in origin. We found the frame at an antiques market and then had a mattress made to order as a standard-size single mattress wouldn't do. Flora's room is much larger and doubles up as a playroom for both girls. It has a large rush mat spread over the wooden floorboards, and baskets of toys and games are stored under the bed and in a large double-fronted cupboard.*

# Making lavender pillows

All of us at Walnuts Farm absolutely adore the scent of lavender and the sense of calm and wellbeing it instills, particularly at bedtime. In late summer, once we've pruned the lavender, we gather it up and dry it over the next few weeks. We then use the aromatic flowers to fill simple lavender bags fashioned from squares of linen or scraps of old fabric.

Lavender used to grow well here on the stony ground alongside the outbuilding, but this year Bella has been ruthless and pulled it all up, as over the years it had become increasingly woody and unproductive. This decrease in vigour is inevitable and is only slowed by a rigorous biannual pruning. Bella has taken cuttings from the old stock but they will take a couple of years to become well established again.

The lavender species that thrive here are *Lavandula angustifolia* 'Hidcote' and 'Munstead', which are fairly hardy and survive our wet winters. Saying that, we planted lavender between the rose bushes along the railing on the south side of the house and the plants have all failed, perhaps because there is a thick subsoil of clay there so the area is less free-draining than others.

**10-15 teaspoons of dried lavender per bag**

**2 rectangles of linen fabric measuring approximately 16 x 12cm/6½ x 5in**

**dressmakers' pins**

**needle**

**thread**

**25cm/10in thin ribbon per bag**

The time to harvest lavender is late summer, when it is pretty dry already. We cut it at the base of the stems, tie it in bunches and then hang it from the porch rafters to dry out. It looks pretty there, and will be completely dry and ready to use within a few weeks. Before making the pillows, strip the lavender buds from the stems with your fingers and discard the stalks. then place the lavender in a bowl until needed.

Place two pieces of linen wrong side to wrong side, pin them together and sew around three sides with small, plain running stitch. Make sure the stitches are small and close together, otherwise pieces of lavender will seep out. Turn the bag right side out and fill it with spoonfuls of lavender. Once it is plump and filled, fold the raw edges in and neatly sew the remaining open side together, then tie the pillow with a length of decorative ribbon.

# The Bathroom

*When we first moved to Walnuts Farm, we inherited a pink 1970s acrylic bathroom suite and lived with this for a few years before we discovered that we could buy a reasonably priced 1930s bath suite complete with pedestal sink, bathtub and close-coupled lavatory.*

The bathroom is now simple and functional and in keeping with our way of living. We have an old English white heritage radiator that blasts out heat, a hot cupboard with shelves above for storing fresh linen, and plain painted boards on the side of the bathtub and floor. The light fitting is a simple white tin shade, which suits our utilitarian aesthetic.

People say you shouldn't hang paintings in a bathroom but we use this space like a gallery and hang our favourite family photos in white box frames. One wall is covered from top to bottom with old photographs and it's a treat to lie in the bath and dream and reminisce.

The bathroom window looks north over the kitchen garden. Thus there is a huge sense of achievement and satisfaction when the kitchen-garden beds are well weeded and at their height of productivity, and a sense of work waiting to be done when not!

# Making calendula salve

Much to Nick's annoyance and Bella's delight, *Calendula officinalis*, commonly known as pot marigold, self-seeds freely in our kitchen garden. Recently we have started making a salve from the flower petals, which Bella picks, crushes and steeps in almond oil for a couple of weeks, before blending the oil with beeswax. It's similar to making furniture polish, but for the skin.

The recipe we use was devised by Carl Legge of *Permaculture* magazine. He attributes calendula salve with having incredible soothing and healing properties for irritated and dry skin. It is also antiseptic and anti-bacterial and is equally effective for treating mild skin conditions and moisturizing older, dry skin.

To make the salve, you'll need a double boiler or bain-marie. (A double boiler can be made by floating a small heatproof glass bowl inside a saucepan filled with hot water.) You will also need some muslin and a sieve or colander over a bowl, to strain the flowers from the oil.

**21 fresh heads of young calendula flowers**

**600ml/2½ cups olive oil or almond oil**

**60g/2oz beeswax chips**

*MAKES 540ml/19fl oz of salve, poured into nine 60ml/2½fl oz glass screw-topped jars*

Pick the heads from young plants, ideally early in the morning on a dry day, just after any dew has evaporated. This ensures the maximum active ingredients are in the oils of the petals. Pull the petals off the flower heads and place in a glass jar. Cover them with the oil. Leave to infuse for two weeks, so the active ingredients in the petals can transfer to the oil.

Strain the oil from the petals into a bowl using the muslin cloth inside a sieve or colander. Squeeze the muslin to get all the oil out. The oil should have taken on the vibrant colour of the calendula flowers.

Put the oil into a small heatproof bowl and place the bowl over gently simmering water. Pour the beeswax chips into the oil and stir gently until the beeswax is melted and thoroughly combined with the oil. The beeswax will help the oil to set into a salve and has soothing properties of its own. Carefully pour the salve into the glass jars and screw on the lids. After a little while, the salve will have set. Store in a cool, dark place.

# The Hallway

*Some sort of entrance hall is desirable as a half-in, half-out space, where guests can be greeted and coats removed. Ours is very small, with barely enough room for one person, but it serves its purpose as an airlock, keeping cold air out and preventing warm air from the adjoining heated rooms from escaping into the night as our guests leave. The reverse is true in the hottest of summers, when we keep doors and windows shut tight during the day, to retain the cool air (and we draw the curtains too, when the sun beats on the window glass).*

Coir floor mats trap the mud, and a thick, interlined curtain against the door keeps winter draughts at bay. It can be removed in summer for a lighter, brighter feel, when we replace it with linen that acts as an insect screen. Glass-fronted cabinets line the walls, where collections of fishing tackle lie in wait to lure us outside and down to the river or sea.

OPPOSITE *A Roger Oates flatweave stair runner quietens footfall on the stairs, and echoes the colours of the living room. The remains of 200 years of paint layers reveal the original lath-and-plaster wall. Above the banister, a Bakelite switch controls illumination.*

ABOVE LEFT AND RIGHT *Fishermen are notorious collectors and this cabinet both stores and displays fly boxes and reels, together with artificial lures and spinning baits plus glass jars holding fly-tying feathers. Opposite, a display shelf holds treasured family photographs.*

# Sources

## UK SOURCES

### Farming supplies and information

**British Beekeepers Association**
bbka.org.uk
*Joining your local beekeeping association is a good idea if you want to get started in beekeeping. They run courses, sell secondhand kit and offer invaluable advice for newcomers.*

**Coronation Meadows**
coronationmeadows.org.uk
*A charitable trust set up to identify, save and restore our ancient flower-rich meadow and grassland in the UK. Very useful for those wishing to create new meadows or restore existing ones.*

**Flowerscapes**
flowerscapes.org.uk
*Specialist wildflower seed mixes designed with bees and other pollinating insects such as butterflies in mind.*

**Hawthbush Farm**
hawthbushfarm.co.uk
*Eco-friendly luxury farm holiday cottages, wild camping and workshops.*

**Kadai Firebowls Charcoal Maker**
kadai.co.uk
*Great little charcoal makers that work brilliantly and make great presents.*

**Mantel Farm**
mantelfarmshop.co.uk
*Suppliers of poultry and beekeeping equipment.*

**Mole Online**
moleonline.com
*Suppliers of all the essential kit for the small farmer and gardener.*

**Small Farm Training Group**
sftg.co.uk
*Based in Sussex, this organization teaches farming, smallholding and horticultural skills.*

**EH Thorne Ltd**
thorne.co.uk
*The best-known suppliers of bees and a full range of beekeeping equipment with a useful mail order catalogue.*

**Verm-X**
verm-x.com
*Verm-X is a blend of 100% natural herbal ingredients for maintaining all areas of intestinal hygiene, offering control and protection. The range contains different formulations for different species.*

**Victoriana Nursery Gardens**
victoriananursery.co.uk
*Nut trees, fruit trees and soft fruit, grape vines and vegetables too.*

**Woodland Trust**
woodlandtrust.org.uk
*This woodland conservation charity gave us a grant to plant 500 native mixed woodland trees.*

## Food and drink

**Abernethy Butter**
abernethybuttercompany.com
*Creamy homemade butter available online.*

**The Garlic Farm**
thegarlicfarm.co.uk
*All types of garlic available online.*

**Gun Brewery**
gunbrewery.co.uk
*Local beer brewed on an organic estate.*

**High Weald Crayfish**
fishandsmith.com
*Contact Kit Smith for orders of Red Signal crayfish caught locally in the High Weald. The season runs from March to November.*

**Homestead Farm**
homestead-farm.co.uk
*Butchery service available from Ivan and Dave for those who rear their own produce.*

**Hook and Son Dairy**
hookandson.co.uk
*Raw organic milk delivered to the door as well as other dairy products.*

**Oxney Organic Estate**
oxneyestate.com
*The best rosé wine you have ever tasted as well as an English sparkling wine, lamb meat boxes and holiday cottages.*

**Weschenfelder**
weschenfelder.co.uk
*Natural sausage casings and skins.*

## Interiors

**Baileys Home**
baileyshome.com
*Suppliers of our simple white 1930s bathroom at a reasonable price.*

**Brickett Davda**
brickettdavda.com
*Simple handmade tableware, glazed in a beautifully muted palette of colours.*

### Firle Place Herb Garden
firle.com
*Beauty balms, teas, soaps, medicinal balms all made from plants and herbs grown in this fabulous garden.*

### Goose Home and Garden
goosehomeandgarden.com
*Vintage finds, such as our folk art farming and animal figures and Beurre Hardy pear sign, and vintage bee hives.*

### Heritage Cast Iron Radiators
heritagecastironradiators.com
*Reconditioned original cast-iron radiators that retain the heat well and look the part.*

### Labour and Wait
labourandwait.co.uk
*Tin lampshades and lots more lovely household goods available online.*

### Objects of Use
objectsofuse.co.uk
*Everyday household tools sourced from around the world.*

### Rushmatters
rushmatters.co.uk
*Traditional rush floor matting made to order. Both beautiful and practical.*

### Stone Age
stone-age.co.uk
*Suppliers of stone flooring as well as the limestone shelves in the pantry and the stone worktop in our kitchen.*

### Wayward
wayward.co
*Vintage fabric and haberdashery.*

## Clothing

### Carhartt Clothing
tkworkwear.com
*The UK suppliers of our favourite US workwear. Carhartt clothing improves with age, softening and fading, and is both comfortable and hardwearing.*

### Carrier Company
carriercompany.co.uk
*Workwear for men and women.*

### Darcy Clothing
darcyclothing.com
*Great practical workwear shirts.*

## US SOURCES

### Hobby Farms
hobbyfarms.com
*All the information needed to start a hobby farm and keep it running smoothly plus an online community of small-scale farmers.*

### Mother Earth News
motherearthnews.com
*Practical skills for modern homesteading and self-sufficient living.*

### American Poultry Association
amerpoultryassn.com

### Backyard Chickens
backyardchickens.com
*Online resource about raising, keeping, and appreciating chickens.*

### Backyard Poultry magazine
backyardpoultrymag.com
*Information on small-flock poultry.*

### The American Livestock Breeds Conservancy
albc-usa.org

### American Beekeeping Federation
abfnet.org
*A national organization with over 1,200 members that continually works in the interest of all beekeepers, large or small.*

### Garden Simply
gardensimply.com
*Website with lots of information on sustainable organic gardening.*

### The Organic Gardener
the-organic-gardener.com
*Growing food and crops organically.*

### Find Native Plants
nwf.org
*State-by-state guide to the native plants for your region.*

### Kitchen Gardeners International
changemakers.com
*Promotes kitchen gardening, home-cooking, and sustainable local food systems.*

### Home Orchard Society
homeorchardsociety.org
*Advice on growing fruit at home.*

### Local Harvest
localharvest.org
*Find farmers' markets, family farms, and other sources of sustainably grown food in your area.*

### American Meadows
americanmeadows.com
*Information on creating a wildflower meadow and supplier of seeds*

### Wildflower Mix
wildflowermix.com
*Information on creating a wildflower meadow and supplier of seeds*

# Index

# Acknowledgments

It would be easy to make the old joke when writing about a home: that "this book is dedicated to [insert your mortgage provider of choice], to whom we are greatly indebted". Instead, we would like to say that this book is dedicated to our fathers; Timothy Serocold Pringle and Ivor Lovell Ivins, who shared many outdoor sporting interests and a love of a good joke. They would have walked the same Mayfair streets although, as far as we know, they never met. Nick would like to make an additional dedication to the late Canadian journalist Robert 'Bobby' Miller who, during the course of many wide-ranging discussions that generally started with modern Anglo-American political and economic history but ended altogether somewhere else, told Nick that he thought perhaps he might write, and also to the teacher of English who told Nick that he certainly could not.

Having thanked those who are no longer with us, Bella would very sensibly like to thank those who are still with us and have been very much part of the making of Walnuts Farm and our homestead.

Thank you to our families and friends, who have supported the restoration of the house and surrounding land at Walnuts Farm when at times the going seemed so tough and the project relentless. Special thanks are due to Pauline Dorchy, Bella's truly inspirational mother, whose great natural sense of style in the many interiors

and gardens she has created in her lifetime has been a huge inspiration and influence. Thank you to our girls, Flora and Peggy, who it has been a pleasure and a privilege to raise at Walnuts Farm, and who are the reason for bringing this special place into being and making it what it is. And to the passing walkers who, unprompted, complimented us upon our work, often at the end of a hard and laborious day when it was difficult for us to see what we had achieved.

Particular thanks for help in the making of this book also go to Jenny and Cliff for extra soft fruits, Loudon and Grania for extra lavender and apple orchards, Alex at Firle Place for her wonderful balms and soaps, our neighbour Charles for use of his lake jetty, the talented Kit for help catching a quantity of crayfish and again to Bella's mother Pauline for supplying us with quantities of dried lavender at the eleventh hour.

But, above all, this book is dedicated to you, dear reader, who upon some whim chanced to pick up this volume. May it inspire you without deterring you, for everything we have done and described here is more than attainable at least in some degree, whether you farm acres of fertile soil or tend the humblest of backyards. And, if you find yourself in the grey concrete jungle (perhaps picking over this book during a hurried lunchbreak), may it lead you to a life beyond it.